CANNAB

First published in the UK in 2018 by ILEX,
a division of Octopus Publishing Group Ltd
Carmelite House
50 Victoria Embankment
London EC4Y 0DZ
www.octopusbooks.co.uk

For Ilex:
Publisher: Roly Allen
Editorial Director: Helen Rochester
Commissioning Editor: Zara Anvari
Managing Editor: Frank Gallaugher
Senior Editor: Rachel Silverlight
Art Director: Julie Weir
Designer: Mónica Oliveira
Senior Production Manager: Peter Hunt

This 2018 edition published by
Hampton Roads Publishing Company, Inc.
Charlottesville, VA 22906
Distributed by Red Wheel/Weiser, LLC
www.redwheelweiser.com

Sign up for our newsletter and special offers by going to
www.redwheelweiser.com/newsletter

ISBN 978-1-57174-846-1

Library of Congress Cataloging-in-Publication Data
available upon request.

Printed and bound in China
Printed by 1010 Printing
10 9 8 7 6 5

This book contains information on growing marijuana:
it has been written and published with the intention of
offering information to the public.

Marijuana is a controlled substance in North America and
throughout much of the world. The publisher does not
advocate the practice of illegal activities and advises the
reader to conduct their own research in order to gain a
thorough understanding of the legal restrictions that may
apply to them.

CANNABIS

a beginner's guide to growing marijuana

DANNY DANKO

Senior Cultivation Editor of
High Times

Foreword by Jorge Cervantes

HAMPTON ROADS

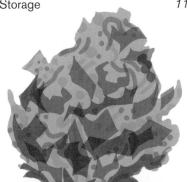

Foreword:
Jorge Cervantes

Danny Danko was my only choice to assume my question-and-answer column for *High Times*. Danny, my protégé and friend, is a dedicated cannabis cultivator. His numerous articles packed with expert advice have helped growers produce crop after crop of outstanding cannabis.

His newest book, *POT: A Beginner's Guide to Growing Marijuana*, gives new growers the exact information they need to grow successful cannabis crops. This work is not filled with fluff and unfounded opinions. It is packed with tried-and-true techniques that produce heavy harvests every crop.

Danny, Senior Cultivation Editor at *High Times*, and I have stood together to present many cultivation seminars at events in North America and Europe. He has developed a deep and intricate knowledge of cultivation practices and techniques. Extensive travel and garden tours have given Danny the ability to write about and demonstrate cultivation practices that growers use around the world. His vast knowledge will help you expand your garden know-how beyond localized methods that often diminish harvest.

Danny and I have toured many gardens together and spent countless hours with expert growers learning and putting into practice bona fide cultivation techniques that work every time. Unlike many authors, Danny has been in the trenches and raised beds of countless gardens. His extensive garden background and contact with growers in the US and around the world, coupled with his direct writing style, provide you with specific information you can apply immediately.

You are smart to follow my lead and invest in Danny's expertise, and draw on his extensive knowledge to grow big buds the first time and every time.

Introduction: Why Grow Your Own?

Why make cannabis cultivation your new hobby? Because you can create a far more superior product, tailor-grown for your medical needs, from seed to harvest, cheaply and effectively, in a relatively small space. Besides this, you'll know everything that went into, or was sprayed onto, your precious buds. If you want to grow organic, or even vegan buds, it's totally up to you.

Lab tests regularly find evidence of pesticides, fungicides, and other potential poisons on commercially grown cannabis. Most pot grown for retail sale is rarely flushed, nor properly dried and cured. Overfeeding runs rampant and the finished product can burn improperly and taste harsh. Some plants are even harvested when immature or overly ripe, decreasing their appeal and effectiveness.

It's also essential to know the genetics of what you're growing and consuming. Different pot strains can vary greatly in flowering time, aroma, flavor, and, most importantly, potency level. Medical marijuana patients must be certain that they're getting the most effective remedy for treating specific ailments and symptoms.

But most of all, growing your own is fun! Like modern-day alchemy, you can conjure connoisseur-quality cannabis with just light, air, water, and food.

The book you hold in your hands is the key to gaining a solid understanding of how pot plants grow and what you'll need to grow them from start to finish. I hope you will embark on this rewarding and never-ending journey using the information and tools provided herein.

Get growing today!
Danny Danko

CHAPTER ONE

Plant Growth Basics
& Grow Room Setup

Gain a basic understanding of the way
that cannabis plants grow and how to
get started on the road to growing
your own pot.

Photosynthesis & the Marijuana Life Cycle

Assuming you've never grown a plant indoors before in your life, let's start from the beginning.

Photosynthesis is the process by which plants convert light, air, and water into the carbohydrate sugars that make up plant cells. The light energy and carbon dioxide (CO_2) absorbed by leaves, and the water taken in by roots, are transformed into glucose, releasing oxygen as a by-product. Plants use the glucose "fuel" to grow new shoots and branches, and they also store the converted energy in their leaves, fruits, flowers, and roots.

Marijuana is an annual, meaning it emerges from a seed in the spring, puts on leaves and branches through the summer, flowers during the fall, and then goes to seed and dies. The fallen seeds, dormant through the winter, sprout in the warming earth of spring. This is as opposed to perennials that live year after year from the same rootstock. In the wild, male cannabis plants pollinate the female flowers through the air to create the seeds, but with domestic and commercial marijuana, breeding is a controlled process.

The buds we consume are the dried flowers of the unpollinated female cannabis plant. Males are useless to anyone but breeders, who collect the pollen from male flowers in order to pollinate female flowers to produce seeds. You may one day want to experiment with creating your own strain, but right now, let's stick to the basics. Generally, for personal pot production, only females should be grown and male plants should be discarded as soon as they're discovered to prevent the seeding of your crop (see Chapter 4).

When growing indoors, we seek to imitate the changing seasons by manipulating the light cycle to trigger the two stages of growth: the vegetative phase and the flowering phase. You can recreate the summer and fall seasons by using a timer on your lighting. The "summer," or vegetative stage, requires 18–20 hours of light per day, and the "fall," or flowering stage needs 12 hours of light and 12 full hours of darkness in order to trigger the plant to develop buds on its branches (see Chapter 7 and Chapter 8 for more on the different growing phases).

A typical vegetative period is 3–4 weeks and flowering generally takes around 8–9 weeks, so plan accordingly. Because you are using artificial light, you can determine the length of the vegetative stage and shorten or extend it according to your space and needs. In addition, your schedule should include a week for drying and a few weeks for curing after this. The best indoor growers keep copious notes and use a calendar to ensure their timing is right.

Essentially, cannabis plants need light, water, fresh air, minerals, and nutrients. Our job as gardeners is to provide our plants with the proper levels of all of these things. Think of them as links of a chain; one broken link and the chain is undone. Dial them all in, and your plants will thrive.

Where to Grow: Room, Tent, or Grow Box?

You need to decide on the location of your garden. A spare bedroom is ideal but an area set aside in your basement or attic could also work. Closets and storage areas are easily converted into small gardens, but you may want to consider a growing tent or grow box. Tents can be set up quickly and come down just as fast, making them a stealthy choice—bear in mind that there are ambiguities in the laws around growing medical marijuana. Secrecy is of utmost importance if you want to avoid any trouble from police, as well as thieves. In addition to the security factor, if you're willing to spend a bit more money you can buy a grow box that allows you to control virtually everything inside with precision. You can monitor ventilation, lighting, and feeding schedules, as well as every other environmental factor, and most look like simple storage units or large toolboxes.

The most affordable way to get started is to purchase a grow tent. These are light-tight units that one person can assemble and take apart. Make sure you choose a tent with sturdy metal supports for your lighting system, and that it is equipped with holes for intake and outtake fans, as well as flood protection in case of any spills.

A grow box is the simplest solution—they provide everything you need in one package—but any box worth having is likely to set you back at least twice the cost of a complete tent installation. It also locks you in to a certain size and setup, which can cause frustration if you decide you want to expand or upgrade.

Grow rooms allow for more customization and maximum spatial efficiency, but it's a fairly permanent setup so it requires an extra level of commitment and planning. I don't recommend it for beginners, but if you do decide to go down this route, consider that you will need to make it light-tight, set up a ventilation system and a lighting system, add heating and air-conditioning units as necessary, and create different spaces for the different growing and harvesting phases. If you want to do it properly, you'll also need to paint the walls or cover them with a reflective surface, and install plumbing according to your needs.

Whichever space you settle on, the same issues tend to apply—lighting, environmental control, and odor control. The deciding factors will be the space you have available, your budget, the amount you want to grow, and concern for secrecy. It's worth reading the rest of this book to gain a better understanding of the whole process before you shell out.

Lighting Your Indoor Grow

Indoor pot cultivation requires some form of artificial lighting. Even a sunny windowsill doesn't provide the amount of sustained light necessary to produce a decent yield of dense cannabis flowers. To determine the type and size of the lighting system that's best for you, two major factors must be considered: the size of the space you're lighting and your ability to control the temperature and humidity in that environment. The lighting systems that produce the largest harvests tend to also generate the most heat. Without the ability to control the temperature, your grow space will become too hot for your plants, resulting in catastrophe. No matter which system you choose, you'll need a quality timer to turn the light on and off every day at the right intervals.

Fluorescents

Fluorescent tubes and CFL (compact fluorescent light) units work decently for growers on a budget, and since they can be kept close to the plants without fear of burning them, they can be handy in small grow spaces.

Tubular fluorescents come in a variety of lengths and widths; look for T5 models. High output (HO) fluoros emit twice as much light as the regular kind, but they also use a lot more electricity.

You can coax nice buds out of plants using fluorescents, but you're unlikely to get the yields that a HID system (see overleaf) can produce.

LED

Advancements in LED (light-emitting diode) technology look very promising, and testing results show that their future is bright. LEDs are extremely efficient so they drastically reduce power consumption and heat, creating usable lumens without the typical drawbacks of other light systems.

As LEDs continue to improve in performance and come down in price, they become more desirable as grow lighting. Still, at this point I recommend them only for use during vegetative growth, or as supplemental lighting to a main HID lighting system.

Reflectors

Reflective units redirect light toward the plants, rather than letting it be wasted on the ceiling and walls of your grow space.

HID

The ultimate lighting system is a high-intensity discharge (HID) light system, either metal halide (MH) or high-pressure sodium (HPS), consisting of an electrical ballast, a bulb, and the reflector housing. Ceramic metal halides (CMH) are the newest grow lights on the scene and have shown much promise in reducing electrical costs and heat produced.

HID lights are most indoor growers' lighting of choice for good reason. A variety of wattages—from 150 watts through 250, 400, and 600 watts, to the mighty 1,000-watt lights—make HIDs versatile as well as unmatched in their ability to deliver the essential lumens needed for plants to thrive inside. A mixture of MH and HPS lights is the ideal, but the prevailing wisdom is that MH lights are better for stacking nodes during the vegetative stage of growth, while HPS lights more closely mimic the golden red glow of fall sunshine, so these are the best choice during the flowering stage.

The downside to HIDs is that they do produce a lot of heat, meaning you will need to find some way of cooling your space, and you should be careful not to burn your crops.

The Setup

Using HIDs, a minimum of 50 watts per square foot (6,000 lumens per square foot) is necessary to maximize growth rates without creating too much heat. Avoid overkill: put 1,000-watt lights in a cupboard and you're giving yourself the unnecessary headache of a lot of hot air to get rid of. Whichever lighting system you opt for, you're aiming for 6,000 lumens minimum.

Remember that you're looking to direct as much light as possible onto your plants. Use the best reflectors you can afford to maximize the light shining on your plants, and hang lights as close as possible to the plants without burning them to avoid lanky, stretched plants.

Ballast

Electrical ballast converts your mains current to the voltage necessary to power your lights. Some systems (like CFLs) have ballast built in, but HID systems will require separate units. You can buy either electromagnetic or digital ballast. The magnetic kind are cheaper, but digital ballasts are cleverer, quieter, and lighter, so I strongly recommend making the investment.

Avoid Light Leaks

Before putting any plants into your space, get inside it with the lights off during the daytime. If you can see any light from outside penetrating through cracks or holes in your space, seal them and try again. Light leaks during the dark cycle of your flowering stage will confuse your plants into staying in the vegetative stage, re-vegging, or even turning into hermaphrodites. Ensure that your dark period will truly all of these calamities from occurring.

How High Should I Hang My Light?

A general rule is around one foot away, but this varies depending on the light of your choice. 1,000-watt HPS lights should be roughly 18 inches from canopy level, while a bank of fluorescent lights can be 3–4 inches from the growing shoots. Too close and you burn your plants; too far away and they stretch due to lack of light. Testing the heat at canopy level on the back of your hand gives a decent guide.

You'll need to adjust the distance (either by raising the lights or lowering the plants) as the plants grow, so factor this into your grow room design.

Soil vs Hydroponics

Growers face their next major choice deciding which medium to grow their plants in. Traditionally, plants are grown in soil or soilless potting mixes that mimic natural earthy loam. Advances in hydroponics—or the growing of plants with their roots immersed in a nutrient solution—allow cultivators to increase the rate of growth as well as final yields. Roots growing in a hydroponic system typically grow bigger plants faster than the same roots in a soil-type medium. On the other hand, growing in soil is just a lot more straightforward and harder to get wrong than hydroponics. When you're growing hydroponically, you are responsible for the plant's every nutritional need, and you have a lot less leeway when it comes to mistakes.

Growing in Soil-Type Mediums

There are many choices of medium but the most popular are peat-based soilless mixes, coco coir, perlite, rockwool, and the expanded clay pellets sometimes referred to as "grow rocks." Whatever medium you choose, it must be loose and airy and allow oxygen to reach your roots.

For beginners, I always recommend growing in a soilless mix or coco coir. These mediums hold roots, yet allow plenty of oxygen to reach them without the typical hassles of hydroponic growing, such as water temperature fluctuations or clogged tubes. Coco coir requires a slightly different nutrient and pH profile, and watering must take place more often than with soil, but I find it to be the best of both worlds and one of the most ecological ways to grow indoors.

The simplest way to get started is to get some five-gallon buckets and fill them with a peat-based soilless mix. Cut holes in the bottom of the buckets for drainage and place trays underneath the buckets to keep the overflow from spilling onto your floor. Never allow the buckets to linger in stagnant water.

What You Need

- × Buckets (5-gallon or larger)
- × Soil mix
- × Watering can

21

Growing Hydroponically

Hydroponics is the art of growing plants without soil. A nutrient solution made up of water and plant foods mixed together in a reservoir is typically fed to the plant roots several times a day. The roots sit in inert mediums such as rockwool, perlite, or grow rocks. Some hydroponic systems such as DWC (deep water culture) employ no growing medium at all; the roots simply dangle in the oxygenated nutrient solution and take up the liquid and foods they need.

Hydro Systems

Nutrient Film Technique (NFT)
NFT uses round or squared tubes with a constant flow of shallow nutrient solution. The roots sit in the trench and take up what they need, eventually forming a mat along the bottom of the tubes. It's important to ensure that the water is well oxygenated because the roots dangle down into the solution.

Ebb & Flow/Flood & Drain
These systems use trays holding plants in their growing mediums. Nutrient solution is periodically pumped into the trays from a reservoir and then drained back into the reservoir to wait for the next feeding cycle. These systems allow the roots to take in plenty of oxygen between waterings.

Deep Water Culture (DWC)
In DWC systems, each plant gets its own bucket, typically five-gallon or bigger. The plants are secured individually in mesh pots cut into the top of the buckets and the roots dangle down into the oxygenated nutrient solution. Unencumbered by a grow medium, roots grow very quickly. Sometimes, the buckets are connected to a larger reservoir, but DWC buckets can also stand alone.

Aeroponics
Plants grown aeroponically are fed their nutrient solution by a mist aimed at the roots. Solution is fed by a pump through misters that bathe the roots constantly, allowing them to absorb food while also taking in abundant amounts of oxygen. When aeroponic methods are dialed in, plants grow incredibly fast and big.

Hydro Mediums

Expanded Clay Pellets

Also known as "grow rocks," clay pellets are heated and then expand, forming what look like solid rocks but actually contain many crevices and air holes for oxygen to circulate. They can be reused many times over as long as they are properly cleaned between cycles.

Rockwool

Rockwool is made from rock that is heated and spun into long fibers that resemble the insulation used in buildings between walls. It has the advantage of holding lots of water while allowing air to reach roots. Rockwool can be an irritant to the skin and lungs, so always get it wet before working with it.

Perlite/Vermiculite

Perlite and vermiculite are two forms of heated minerals that expand into small porous pebbles. They are typically used to lighten soilless mixes but can also be used alone as hydroponic mediums. Both exhibit good water retention and also have "wicking" properties that draw nutrient solution upward.

Coco Coir/Coco Peat

Coco coir or peat, made from the fibers on the outside of a coconut shell, is a natural medium that's the by-product of the coconut industry. Many hydroponic growers enjoy using this medium over rockwool due to its sustainability and water-retention abilities. This medium requires a unique and specific type of nutrient solution made especially for use with coco.

What You Need

- ✕ Growing tray or tubes
- ✕ Grow medium
- ✕ Reservoir for nutrient solution
- ✕ Water pump with a timer for nutrient solution
- ✕ Air pump and air stones to oxygenate solution
- ✕ pH meter to measure the acidity or alkalinity of solution
- ✕ TDS meter to measure the concentration of nutrient salts in solution

23

Food & Water

Watering

Your chosen medium will help determine how often you water and feed your plants. Cannabis roots generally prefer a balanced wet and dry cycle rather than being constantly soaked or perennially parched. Over-watering and over-fertilizing are the two biggest mistakes that novice growers make, so try to create a balance. Lift your containers when they're fully watered and when you know that they're not to gain a sense of how heavy they feel, and you will soon learn to tell when they need another watering.

In areas with particularly poor water, a reverse osmosis (RO) filtration system may be needed to remove impurities. Never use cold or hot water as this can shock roots. Between 65–80 degrees Fahrenheit is the ideal temperature for water. Use a thermometer to make sure you're getting it right.

PPM

PPM or Parts Per Million is the measure of mineral solubles in water. Get a TDS meter and test the runoff water regularly to get a grasp of normal levels and catch irregularities quickly.

pH Level

The pH level is a measurement of the acidity or alkalinity of your nutrient solution or growing medium. It takes the form of a scale from 0–14, with 0 being the most acidic and 14 the most alkaline. With a soilless mix, you should strive for a pH level of 6.0–6.5—just slightly on the acidic side of neutral 7.0. For hydroponic growers, the pH of their nutrient solution should be slightly lower (between 5.5 and 6.2) Fluctuations in pH cause nutrients to be locked out and unable to be absorbed by roots. All water or nutrient solution applied to your plant roots must be adjusted to the proper parameters at all times for healthy growth.

Feeding

Plants need nutrients in different amounts at all stages of life for optimum growth. From seedlings into the vegetative stage and through the flowering period, plants must be fed with fertilizers in different amounts based on their requirements at that time. Some mediums already contain fertilizers, but even those will eventually be used up or washed out and new ones must be added by feeding your plants with nutrients added to the water.

NPK

The three most important compounds plants require are nitrogen (N), phosphorus (P), and potassium (K). These are listed on plant-food packaging as an NPK rating. This rating provides you with an understanding of the nutrient content in a particular bottle as a percentage, therefore an NPK ratio of 10-1-1 will have more nitrogen, and one that reads 1-5-5 has more phosphorus and potassium. These ratios determine which food to give plants during the different stages of growth.

Nitrogen promotes vigorous foliar growth and new plant tissue, while phosphorus encourages the development of roots and flowers. Potassium, or potash, boosts overall plant health and vigor. During vegetative growth, plants require food with a higher nitrogen content, while plants that are blooming need more phosphorus and potassium. (See also Chapter 10 for how to spot deficiencies.)

Micronutrients

In addition to the macronutrients mentioned above, there are also many micronutrients that are necessary for proper plant growth. These include calcium, magnesium, sulfur, and others that must be present, some even in tiny amounts, for plants to thrive. These can be applied as additives to the base nutrients depending on your feeding regimen. Plants also need carbon, hydrogen, and oxygen, but they get these from air and water.

Avoid Overfeeding

The most important thing to remember about nutrients is to avoid overfeeding your plants. It's easy to add more nutrients if you see a deficiency starting, but much harder to remove them once they've been applied. Burned leaf tips (when the tips start to turn yellow-brown) are a sure sign of overfeeding. It's always best to raise nutrient dosages incrementally in order to avoid overdoing it, but if you do see symptoms, flush your plant's root zone with plenty of plain water and check for signs of healthy growth before you re-apply a lower dose of food.

Environmental Controls

Above all, understanding how to control the environment is the single most differentiating factor between the fruitful indoor pot producer and the ones who never seem to get it quite right. Frigid cold or searing heat does serious damage to sensitive plant tissues. A bone-dry humidity level or overly moist atmosphere can cause serious problems quickly, and many times plant death is the result. Even those that don't perish will never be the same again. If you plan to cultivate cannabis without considering how to maintain a proper growing environment inside, you can expect diminishing returns.

Temperature

The goal is to maintain air temperature inside your grow space at 70–80 degrees Fahrenheit. You can let temperatures drop to around 65 degrees at night, but temperatures should never exceed 80 degrees. If high heat is an issue, you will need to find a way to lower it.

Some lighting systems are available in air-cooled versions that remove heat directly from the reflectors at bulb level and can drop temperature at canopy level. An air-conditioning unit, either in a window or freestanding, will also bring down heat levels. Growers in colder climates may need a heater during the dark period to keep temperatures from getting too low.

Humidity

Try to keep humidity between 40–60 percent. Higher humidity levels (70–80 percent) are ideal for cloning and the early seedling stage of growth, but must be brought down to around 50 percent during the vegetative and flowering phases.

A digital thermometer and hygrometer are essential equipment for gauging your temperature and humidity levels. The best units not only track levels at all times but can also tell you the highs and lows during the times when you aren't inside the grow space by sending the data to your mobile device.

Humidity Control

You can regulate the humidity in your grow space with any or a combination of the following, according to your needs:

× Increase/decrease ventilation to make the space less or more humid

× Trim excess foliage to increase air circulation and decrease humidity

× Add or remove water in the space to increase/ decrease humidity

× Adjust the temperature: higher temperatures means greater humidity

× Introduce a humidifier/ dehumidifier into the space

Circulate Air

Moving air around your grow space as well as removing the warm spent and stinky air is essential to successful indoor farming. Oscillating fans should ensure that all growing leaves wiggle in the wind without getting completely blasted by a constant, excessive breeze. An exhaust fan, located near the top of your grow space, pulls air through an activated charcoal filter in order to clean it before setting it free. Pulling more air out than you have flowing in creates negative pressure, ensuring a fresh supply of carbon dioxide and also making certain that odors won't escape through any cracks. Be sure to turn off oscillating fans before any spraying or foliar feeding to avoid getting liquid on your light bulbs, which can deteriorate or break from contact with droplets.

Safety, Security, & Odor Control

Above all, your freedom and health are your most important priorities. Never grow in a location that you feel is compromised. Learn the basics of electrical usage and safety and place an emphasis on suppressing telltale scents that may emanate from your grow space.

Electricity

Electricity is dangerous and growers must have a decent grasp of the risks and limitations of their electrical usage. It's important not to overburden your circuit breakers, so do some research on the relationship between electrical power (watts), current (amps), and voltage (volts), and plan your setup before you run it. Never exceed the recommended amount of current for your electrical equipment.

Air Filtration

All the air that's removed from your grow space with a ventilation fan must go through an activated charcoal filtration system to remove odors. Other products that mask odors are available, but filtration is essential to cleaning the air of smells. Purchase a vent fan with a CFM (cubic feet per minute) rating that will remove and replace all of the air in your room within five minutes. Attach it to the charcoal filter so that all spent air passes through, and replace the charcoal as necessary to continue to efficiently eliminate smells.

Suppressing Noise & Vibration

Lighting system ballasts, fans, and pumps all create noise. (Keep warm ballasts outside of your grow space if possible to decrease built-up heat.) Fans and pumps should be secured and mounted on rubber pads between wood and metal surfaces, when possible. You can buy silencers, or build one yourself, to dampen the noise of fans. Bends in ducting and tubing cause noise and decrease efficiency. Keep ducts as straight as possible to avoid disturbing the flow of your fans.

CHAPTER TWO

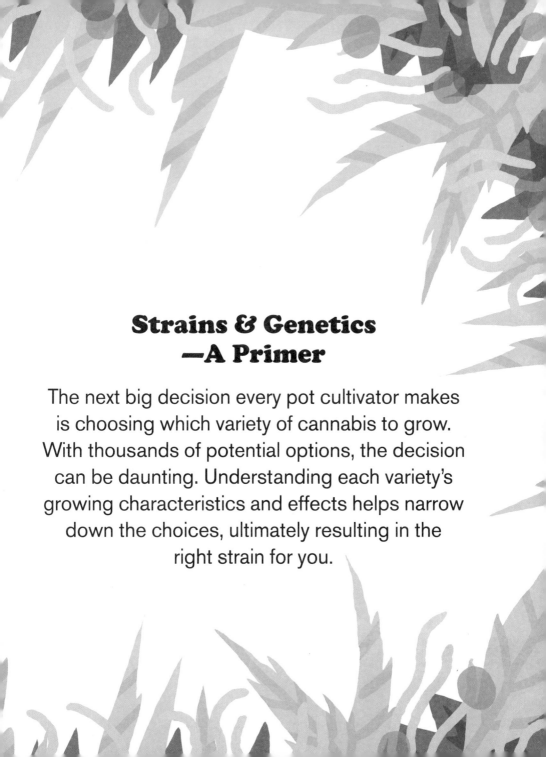

Strains & Genetics —A Primer

The next big decision every pot cultivator makes is choosing which variety of cannabis to grow. With thousands of potential options, the decision can be daunting. Understanding each variety's growing characteristics and effects helps narrow down the choices, ultimately resulting in the right strain for you.

What are Strains & How are they Different?

Strains are the different varieties of marijuana that are available to growers and consumers. Cannabis originated in the Yunnan province of China and then was spread throughout the world by traders on the Silk Road. Over time, as the plant disseminated from Central Asia to the rest of the planet, it adapted to the new environments by acclimatizing to latitude, longitude, and altitude. As a result of these transformations, pot plants from varying regions developed some very different characteristics over centuries. These territorial heirloom varieties are known as landraces and make up the genetic building blocks of the thousands of strains in the marketplace today.

The cannabis consumed now can be generally classified as *indica*, *sativa*, or, most often, a hybrid—a combination of the two subspecies. *Cannabis ruderalis* is a low-THC hemp variety native to Eastern Europe and Russia, which grows wild and is used to breed auto-flowering strains.

Different strains express different characteristics, including speed of growth and size of the full-grown plant, the shape of the leaves and flowers, the amount of time it takes for buds to ripen, potency and cannabinoid composition, and many other factors. For as long as cannabis has been cultivated, breeders have been working to bring out the properties they desire through a gradual process of crossbreeding and refining over generations, until they achieve a genetically stable archetype.

Today there are thousands of strains to choose from, none quite the same as another. When it comes to choosing a strain to grow yourself, you'll want to consider factors such as hardiness, size, and ease of cultivation, as well as the qualities you're looking for in the end product that you'll consume, such as size of harvest, potency, and a cannabinoid and terpene composition suitable for your medical needs (see page 39).

Indicas

Indicas were originally acclimated to the mountainous Hindu Kush region and are typically thought of as Afghani, Kashmiri, or Kush. Asian *indica*-dominant strains include Hindu Kush, Mazar-i-Sharif, South Indian Kerala, Chitrali, Taskenti, Nepali Highland, Pakistani, and Uzbek. In the Middle East, Lebanese Hash Plant as well as Syrian and Egyptian strains are the traditional hash-making landrace varieties.

Indicas are characterized by their short stature and wide leaf structure. Traditionally, these plants were grown and bred for making hashish and the buds are covered with glandular trichomes that are sometimes referred to as "crystals" or "kif." The trichomes are sifted away from the leaf and buds, and then pressed to make hashish. *Indicas* have short flowering times, typically between 45 and 60 days, as opposed to *sativa*-dominant strains that tend to flower for 60 days or longer. This and their smaller size makes them somewhat easier to grow than *sativa* varieties. *Indicas* tend to have high cannabidiol (CBD) contents and give their users a lethargic, relaxed feeling.

For medicinal patients, *indicas* are thought to be effective in treating anxiety, pain, nausea, insomnia, muscle spasms, and tremors, among other symptoms.

Favorite *Indica*-Dominant Strains

- ✗ OG Kush
- ✗ Grape Ape
- ✗ Blueberry
- ✗ Lavender
- ✗ Cheese

Sativas

Sativas are now native to the Indian subcontinent, but are also grown in Southeast Asia, South and Central America, the Caribbean, and Africa. Among the many landrace *sativas* from Southeast Asia are Lowland and Highland Thai, Vietnamese, Burmese, Cambodian, and Laotian. Central and South American *sativas* include Panama Red, Acapulco Gold, Oaxacan Highland, Zacatecas Purple, Santa Marta Gold, Punta Roja, and Brazilian. *Sativas* from the African continent include Malawi Gold, Durban Poison, Nigerian, Swazi Red, Swazi Skunk, and Congolese. Hawaiian varieties such as Maui Wowie and Kona Gold round out the list.

Sativas are the taller, longer-flowering variety native to equatorial regions with a longer growing season. The leaves are typically thinner and longer than those of *indicas*, and the buds tend to be thinner and more elongated as well, with longer distances between nodes on the branches. *Sativa* plants were traditionally bred for hemp purposes as well as for medicinal applications, and they have less bulbous trichomes than *indicas*. With a THC content that is relatively unopposed by THC-regulating CBD, *sativas* produce psychedelic effects, and a characteristic *sativa* high is known to be racy and "electric." The product of some pure *sativas* have been known to induce paranoia and heart-racing in unsuspecting smokers.

Growing *sativas* is an exercise in patience. They take longer to flower than *indicas* and tend to give smaller yields. Medicinally, *sativas* are believed to soothe depression, ADD, and fatigue, while also increasing appetite.

Favorite *Sativa-Dominant* Strains

× Strawberry Cough
× Jack Herer
× Kali Mist
× Blue Dream
× Dr. Grinspoon
× Anything with Haze in the name (e.g. Super Silver Haze)

Hybrids

Hybrids are a combination of *indica* and *sativa* genetics. Because of their different properties, many connoisseurs consider *sativas* to be a daytime smoke and *indicas* primarily a nightcap—but the truth is that most of what is smoked is a hybrid of the two; typically not more than 60 percent of one over the other. Selective breeding allows growers to produce the results they desire in terms of just about everything, from the size and yield of a plant to the flavor and type of high.

The ideal hybrids exhibit the best characteristics of both, like the shorter flowering times and stocky stature of an *indica* combined with the uplifting high and flavorful terpene profile of a *sativa*. The medical benefits will likewise vary according to the makeup.

Growing *indica*-dominant hybrids indoors is typically easier than *sativa*-dominant ones because of several factors. The shorter flowering time of *indicas* gives you less time to make mistakes and they tend to yield more as well. Also, *indicas* tend to be heavy feeders of nutrients, so they are harder to overfeed than their finicky *sativa* counterparts. In growth, *sativas* also tend to stretch much more, even after flowering is induced, which can cause issues in small spaces.

Favorite Hybrids

- ✗ Girl Scout Cookies
- ✗ Gorilla Glue #4
- ✗ Kali Mist
- ✗ Lemon Skunk
- ✗ Gelato

Choosing the Right Strain for You

Medicinal cannabis users should note that certain strains work better for their malady or symptoms. Pot aficionados know that different hybrids exhibit unique characteristics of flavor, scent, and intoxication. The effects of strains of cannabis vary greatly from catatonic to giddy, and from stoned to high. Personal preference plays an enormous role, and people repeatedly continue to breed the cannabis they most enjoy.

Once you've found the strains you love, you can keep growing them over and over from clones, as long as you create a motherplant of your chosen variety (see Chapters 5 and 6). It's nice to have a selection of different varieties to choose from based on mood and medical needs.

A relatively new development in medicinal cannabis strain breeding is the demand by patients for varieties high in CBD (cannabidiol), a non-psychoactive cannabinoid with efficacious properties. New high-CBD strains are being developed and are sought after by patients suffering from body injuries, severe spasms, or restless leg syndrome. Recent studies have indicated that CBD-rich strains can inhibit the growth of cancer cells and help quell epileptic fits and THC-induced anxiety.

CBD-Rich Strains

× Cannatonic
× Harlequin
× Dinamed CBD
× ACDC
× Ringo's Gift

CHAPTER THREE

Germination—Getting Started

A successful start leads to healthier plants in the future, so it's essential to get your seeds sown properly.

Seeds: Regular, Feminized, & Auto-Flowering

Three different types of seeds are available these days. Recent advancements in breeding have led to changes in how certain plants will perform and what traits they'll exhibit. Varieties have been developed to simplify the growing process and understanding the differences will help you decide on the type of seeds you will acquire and germinate.

Regular Seeds

Because cannabis is dioecious, seeds that have developed with no artificial interference (otherwise known as "regular seeds") will turn out to be either male or female at about a fifty-fifty rate. It's impossible to tell the gender of the seeds without growing them out. Therefore, if you're growing from regular seeds, you need to plant roughly twice the number of seeds to result in the number of female plants you wish to harvest.

Regular seeds from a reputable breeder should be stable F1 hybrids (F1 stands for "first filial generation" and means stable, reliable results—the genetic makeup of the grown plants is constrained). The advantage to growing hybrid plants from regular seeds is that they exhibit what's known as "hybrid vigor"—a tendency to grow stronger than even their parents in the first filial generation. This genetic vitality produces a hardy plant with greater resistance to pests and diseases, and bigger and more potent eventual yields.

Use regular seeds to find your keeper motherplant. Feminized seeds are more prone to hermaphroditism and don't grow with the same vigor to produce healthy cuttings. (See Chapter 5 for more information about motherplants.)

Pros & Cons

× Tend to grow hardier plants

× Hybrids grown from regular seeds grow faster and stronger

× No way to tell the plant's sex before it's grown out

× Twice as many seeds need to be planted

Pros & Cons

- ✗ Guaranteed female plants
- ✗ Saves time
- ✗ Greater possibility of plants turning out to be hermaphrodites

Feminized Seeds

Feminized seeds are made using pollen from a hermaphroditic female plant to pollinate a female plant. Over generations, breeders can create seeds that produce plants with no male chromosome and so the seeds reliably grow into female plants, making it a simple and efficient solution for growers who want to germinate only females in their garden.

The reason people grow plants from feminized seeds is to avoid wasting time and space growing out any undesirable males. If a male grown from regular seeds goes undetected for too long and releases pollen into the garden, an entire crop can go to seed. In Europe, where most growers grow from seeds and not clones, 90 percent of the seeds sold are feminized, so growers never have to seek out males to cull.

This convenience comes with a caveat: some of the plants can turn out to be hermaphrodites if they have questionable genetics. It's true that plants grown from regular seeds can also be hermies, but it's far less common, and typically due to stress such as light leaks or major fluctuations in their environment. You can make mother-plants out of feminized seeds but I don't recommend it.

Auto-Flowering Seeds

Auto-flowering plants are plants that begin the blooming process when they reach a certain height, rather than by any changes in photoperiod, meaning that plants grown from auto-flowering seeds will begin flowering regardless of whether they get 12 hours of light per day or 20. Advancements are improving auto-flowering plants, resulting in larger yields and higher potency levels.

Auto-flowering strains have a *ruderalis* parent somewhere in their genetic makeup, making for hardy plants, if tending to be smaller and with smaller yields than *indica* and *sativa* hybrids. Growers using these genes simply plant their seeds, walk away, and then return in 80 or so days to harvest. No muss, no fuss, no molds. Harvest early using these seeds and you defeat pests and botrytis all at once. You can also harvest more often using auto-flowerers due to their shorter grow schedule, and since the plants stay lower to the ground they can be a good, stealthy option.

Outdoor growers in high altitudes or northern latitudes need strains that can handle the rugged weather and short growing season, and auto-flowering strains do the trick.

Pros & Cons

- ✗ Fuss-free with no need to worry about lighting schedules
- ✗ Small plants are stealthier
- ✗ Hardy plants resistant to pests and diseases
- ✗ Short growing schedules mean more frequent harvests
- ✗ Smaller plants mean smaller yields

Indoors, I recommend a lighting phase of 20 hours on/4 hours off throughout both the vegetative and flowering stages of auto-flowering strains. At 18/6 or any less light, there will be much more stretching and long distances of stem between nodes and branches.

Selecting & Ordering Seeds

If you plan to grow from seeds, you must choose and procure them with enough time to get them started.

Take a look at some reputable seed breeders' websites or catalogs to get an idea of your options. Another great resource is my first book, *The Official High Times Field Guide to Marijuana Strains* (2011) or the hightimes.com website.

Find a trustworthy seed company that's been around for a while and is known in the community, preferably one with plenty of favorable online reviews. Since 2007, I've been compiling our "High Times Seed Bank Hall of Fame" with 50 of the most well-known and respected breeders listed. Check out the entire list at hightimes.com/SeedBankHOF.

Never have seeds shipped to the location at which you plan to grow. Beginners growing indoors should consider an *indica*-dominant strain that will stay relatively smaller and have a shorter flowering time than a *sativa*-dominant variety that can stretch and take longer to reach maturity.

Only use new seeds: seeds that have been sitting around for a while may not germinate at all, and if they do they can be slow to grow and weak, which makes them an attractive target for pests and diseases. The best seeds will be hard and uncracked.

Once you've accounted for unwanted males and weaker plants, you might expect about a quarter of the seeds you planted to grow to maturity, so take this into account and sow accordingly.

Sprouting Seeds

Here I'm going to take you through a simple and effective technique for growing seedlings that will thrive from the very beginning of their lives.

There are several ways to properly germinate seeds. Some people place them between two moistened paper towels and then wait until they start popping open before gently placing them into their growing medium. Two important things to remember if using this technique: don't let the emerging root get too long before planting, and be sure to place the seedling into your growing medium with the taproot pointing downward.

The easiest and most fail-proof way to sow seeds is directly into your growing medium of choice. Poke a hole in your moistened soilless mix (or coco coir, rockwool cube, etc.) and drop the seed in at about a quarter- to half-inch deep. Cover the seed with more mix and keep it moist and warm. It doesn't hurt to put some clear plastic wrap over your container to maintain humidity at the surface of your medium. In a few days, you should see a tiny green shoot emerging from the medium. Immediately place it under adequate (but not too hot) grow lighting and your seedling will stay strong without stretching.

Always take care to maintain the strictest sanitation standards with your delicate seedlings—you should at all times anyway, but a fungal infestation at this stage can lay low a whole crop. Keep your grow room clean, start with a good-quality medium and clean containers, wash your hands before handling, and your seedlings should get off to a good, strong start.

Seedling Care

Young pot plants need extra attention during the earliest growth stage in order to successfully bear fruit down the road.

Lighting for Seedlings

As soon as you see the tiny green shoot coming out from your medium, get the seedling under a grow light. Regular incandescent bulbs will not do so you must consider other options. Determining which type and wattage of lights to use really depends upon the area you've reserved for your garden. HIDs are overkill for micro-grows inside a cabinet or small fridge, but fluorescents aren't ideal for an 8 x 8-foot room. Heat production and electrical costs can also be limiting factors, so choose wisely, being sure to tailor your light to your space. (See also Chapter 1 for information on lighting.)

Young plants don't need such intense light as they will, but if your seedlings appear to be stretching, it's probably because they don't have enough light. You may need to move your lights closer or add extra lights.

No matter which lighting system you choose, you must set it with a vegetative stage light cycle—18–20 hours of light per day. While some growers advocate it, I personally don't recommend a 24-hour-on lighting schedule for vegetating plants. They need at least a few hours of darkness to process the light energy and water they take in during daylight hours. This is when they actually grow. I recommend an 18-hour-on/6-hour-off lighting schedule for areas where heat and electrical costs can be an issue, and 20-hours-on/4-hours-off if heat and expenses aren't a problem. Either way, don't change the lighting schedule once you've decided on one until it's time to flower your plants.

Watering & Feeding Seedlings

If your seedlings were sown in a small container, plug, or rockwool cube, you will want to gently transplant them into a larger container before their root systems get too big. You don't want your young plant to become root-bound and slow its rate of growth. (See Chapter 7 for a step-by-step guide to transplantation).

Marijuana plants prefer a wet and almost-dry cycle so be careful not to overwater your seedlings. Lift them up in their containers to determine by their weight whether they're well watered or getting dry. Water with pH-balanced (6.0–6.5) plain water or a very mild nutrient solution. Keep in mind that the dietary needs of young plants are fairly low. They don't have a lot of roots to take in food, nor do they have much of an actual plant structure to support.

Also, some growing mediums already have some nutrients added to them.

With this in mind, remember that less is more. If your seedlings look healthy and the new and older growth remains a vibrant green, continue watering with plain water or a very mild nutrient solution. If you see the leaves begin to fade from green to a lighter green, or any other sign of deficiency (see Chapter 10), bump up the amount of fertilizer. Continue to use quarter- to half-strength nutrients until the seedling is 6–8 inches tall with several sets of leaves. It's always easier to add more nutrients than it is to remove an overabundance of them.

Seedling Tip

Be sure to label all of your seedlings. This way, you'll be sure to avoid confusion and mistakes down the road.

Temperature & Humidity for Seedlings

Seedlings require more heat and humidity than they will need later in their growth cycles.

Your vegetative space for seedlings should be kept warm (70–75 degrees Fahrenheit), humid (relative humidity near 50 percent), and clean. A good thermometer/hygrometer combo will let you know your temperature and humidity levels at all times so you can act accordingly to maintain them. Depending upon the climate where you live, you may need to add a heater or air-conditioner to control air temperature, and a humidifier or dehumidifier to control the moisture level in your air (see more on humidity in Chapter 1).

After a few weeks, foliage will suddenly and rapidly start sprouting. This is the beginning of the vegetative growth phase that we'll cover in detail in Chapter 7.

CHAPTER FOUR

Sexing Male or Female

Since only female plants produce the resin-covered flowers we desire, males and hermaphrodites must be spotted and eliminated as soon as possible to avoid filling up your buds with seeds.

Determining Plant Sex

The buds we consume are the dried flowers of the unpollinated female cannabis plant. Males are useless to anyone but breeders, who collect the pollen from male flowers in order to pollinate female flowers to produce seeds. You may one day want to experiment with creating your own strain, but right now, let's stick to the basics. Generally, for personal pot production, only females should be grown and male plants should be discarded as soon as they're discovered to prevent the seeding of your crop.

Is it possible to determine the plant's sex while it's still in seed form? Unless the seeds come from suppliers who specifically breed feminized seeds, this isn't possible. Plants must be grown out to determine whether they're males or females. A close look at your plants as they begin the flowering process will reveal their sex.

The flowering process for both males and females begins when plants are exposed to complete darkness for 12 or more continuous hours per day. Indoors, the photoperiod is controlled by the grower, who sets the timer for a 12-hour-on/12-hour-off daily lighting schedule; outdoors, the sun's diminishing rays in early fall trigger cannabis to bloom. Flowers will begin to indicate themselves about a week or two into the flowering cycle. *Indicas* show sex sooner than *sativas*, so be patient with the longer-flowering varieties. Males tend to stretch and grow taller than females, so if you notice this behavior you might want to keep a particular eye on those plants—but alone it isn't a reliable factor for determining plant gender.

Hermaphrodites

Beware the dreaded plant that shows signs of both sexes. These must be discovered and destroyed to avoid filling your flowers with seeds.

When a plant shows both male and female flowers, it's considered a hermaphrodite and should be immediately removed from the garden. Whether you find a use for them, or toss them into a compost pile, get rid of them as soon as you discover them. There are some unstable *sativas* that will show male flowers late into flowering. The yellow male "bananas" that pop out from almost fully formed buds can be removed as they're found and will do little damage at this late stage.

Sinsemilla

Literally meaning "without seeds," sinsemilla is the prize you're after. In order for female buds to be seedless, they must never be pollinated by a male plant. This is why it's so important to discard any male plants as soon as you've detected them. If they release their pollen onto your female plants, your harvest will end up being infested with practically worthless seeds instead of the pristine nuggets you're after.

Female
Keep an eye out for frondy
stigma emerging at the nodes.

Preflowers

Even before flowering, some tiny clues on your plants can
help you gain an understanding of what they may become
when blooming.

Experienced growers can sometimes recognize the sex of their
plants earlier than the flowering period. When propagated from
seeds, plants will begin to show preflowers after a month or so
of vegetative growth. These appear in the middle of the joint, or
node, where individual branches protrude from the main stem.

Male
Male preflowers are round,
ball-shaped sacks, also
observed on the nodes.

Use a loupe or magnifying glass and good lighting to examine the
node. Keep in mind that both sexes will show stipules, the leafy
spikes that protrude from each node. Above the stipule is where
tiny preflowers emerge.

Females indicate themselves with stigma, or fuzzy white hairs,
that extend outward from a teardrop-shaped bract (also known
as a calyx). Male preflowers don't have pistils; they resemble a
closed fist at the end of a very short arm. Some liken them to
mushrooms or to a ball-on-a-stick shape. If you're not sure about
the preflowers, wait it out—there won't be any damage done
at this point. You have plenty of time to become certain before
doing anything drastic, like killing off all suspected males.

Female Flowers

Female flowers begin as tiny white-haired puffballs at branch tips that fill out and stack up as the plant matures.

Female flowers start to show as bracts at the various bud sites that occur at branch nodes and tips. Two white hairs (stigmas) will emerge from the end of the pear-shaped bracts, looking very much like their precursor female preflowers. The bracts gradually swell, becoming covered in a "resin" made up of glandular trichomes—the tiny cannabinoid-containing crystals that glisten like diamonds in the light. As the female flowers mature, thousands of these swelling bracts form into clusters, eventually filling branches to form long colas. Kept free of male pollen and fed with the finest in phosphorus-rich nutrients, females will swell in size, producing trichome-laden buds.

Male Flowers

Male flowers look like tiny yellow bunches of bananas that eventually open up to release their pollen.

A week or two into flowering, when males truly begin to show, they'll look like a miniature bunch of bananas hanging down as they slowly beginning to swell with pollen. You have less than a week to remove the males from your garden at this point, before they release their pollen and seed your entire crop.

If you're interested in experimenting with seed breeding on your own, keep the males alive in a separate area well away from the females. They don't need to thrive—just keep them alive with fluorescents or low-watt grow lights. Place paper under the plants when the male flowers look close to popping open. Once you've collected the pollen, place it in a dry, sealed container. Lightly sprinkle or brush the male pollen onto developing female flowers to create seeds for future crops. Beginner growers shouldn't experiment with breeding, so when in doubt, remove the males upon determining their sex and get rid of them immediately.

CHAPTER FIVE

Motherplants
—Why & How

In order to root and grow clones, you need to have a motherplant from which to take cuttings. Motherplants are females grown from seed and kept in the vegetative stage as needed. Motherplants preserve your preferred genetics, allowing you to grow the same strain over and over again.

Starting Motherplants

Motherplants start as seedlings and grow in the vegetative stage until they're big enough to take clones from.

The best way to acquire a motherplant is to grow one out from seed—but the only way to know the sex of the plant without flowering it (unless it's grown from feminized seeds) is to root a clone from the plant and then flower the clone. The motherplant stays under 18–20 hours of light per day, while the rooted clone corresponding to the plant is placed in a separate flowering area under a 12-hours-on/12-hours-off schedule.

Within two weeks or so, you'll begin to see signs of sex on the clone, but it's best to continue flowering out the clone completely in order to ensure she's not a hermaphrodite. Any signs of male genitalia on your flowering clone mean you must get rid of both the clone and the corresponding motherplant or risk seeding your crops. Remember: male flowers look like tiny bananas sticking out from the buds.

If the clone is female, the corresponding motherplant will also be female, and yet hasn't ever been flowered itself. This means the plant will be free from stress, without ever having its lighting schedule shortened or interrupted. Motherplants grown from already flowered-and-then-reversed plants tend to give off stressed-out (so weaker) cuttings, while motherplants that have stayed in their vegetative stage only give healthy, strong clones.

Motherplant Step by Step

What You'll Need

- ✗ Sharp non-serrated blade or razorblade
- ✗ Propagation tray and clear plastic dome
- ✗ Electric heating pad (propagation mat)
- ✗ Preferred medium (rockwool, soil mix, coco coir, etc.)
- ✗ Rooting hormone (gel or powder)
- ✗ Fluorescent lighting
- ✗ pH-balanced (6.0–6.5) mild nutrient solution
- ✗ Thermometer/ hygrometer

STEP 1

Plant seeds

Plant the seeds from which you will choose your motherplants.

Though it may be tempting to use feminized seeds, my recommendation is to use regular seeds, which will grow into male or female plants. (See Chapter 3 to get your plants off to the best possible start.)

STEP 2

Take clones

Once the seedlings have sprouted and formed at least three sets of leaves, take a clone from each seedling and label the seedlings and their corresponding clones in order to differentiate between them. (See Chapter 6 for step-by-step instructions of how to take cuttings.)

STEP 3

Root the clones

Root the clones under a flowering light schedule (12 hours on/12 hours off) while keeping the corresponding seedlings under a vegetative light schedule (20 hours on/4 hours off).

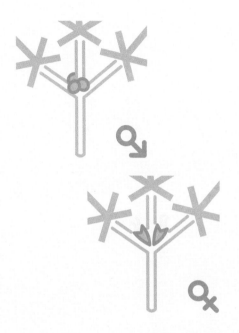

STEP 4

Flower the clones to determine sex and choose a motherplant

After the clones root, they will begin to show their sex. Continue flowering the female clones to determine which ones you wish to keep as motherplants. Determining factors will include flowering time, scent, flavor, and potency.

STEP 5

Discard the male clones and plants

Get rid of the male clones and the corresponding male plants. Keep the seedling or seedlings that correspond to your favorite female flowered clones and these are your new motherplants. Clones from these plants will all exhibit the same qualities.

Choosing a Motherplant

The rooted clones of your motherplants will reveal their sex, growing characteristics, flavor, aroma, and potency, so you'll know what to expect without ever having to flower the moms.

In theory, if you planted 10 regular seeds, you'll be end up with on average five males, and five female potential motherplants. Having discarded the male clones and plants, you now need to examine the female seedlings and their corresponding clones more closely, and choose the phenotype you will hopefully be growing for generations to come. By "phenotype" we mean the combined characteristics expressed by genetic and environmental factors. Once you find the clone with the traits you're looking for, the corresponding vegetating plant becomes the motherplant from which you'll take clones to fill your flowering chamber.

What to Look for in a Motherplant

- ✗ Stability: the plant you choose must not have any hermaphroditic tendencies
- ✗ Potency: choose the plant with the greatest trichome production
- ✗ Aroma and flavor: decide on the plant that smells and tastes the way you like

Motherplant Maintenance

Motherplants can be kept in their vegetative stage for years and provide thousands of rooted cuttings—as long as they remain healthy and strong. It's best to keep your motherplants under metal halide HID lighting, but compact fluorescents or LEDs will work in a pinch.

Feed motherplants a mild vegetative nutrient solution and always monitor it for overfeeding. Diluted formulations of liquid seaweed, liquid fish, and seabird guano are wonderful organic nutrients for motherplants. Because they live much longer lives, motherplants are at a greater risk of deficiencies, nutrient overloads, and pH imbalances. Give them plain pH-balanced and filtered water between feedings and you'll find them much healthier and happier.

Keeping your motherplant alive for multiple cloning sessions requires a bit of planning. Larger containers are necessary for the root systems. Also, motherplants shouldn't enter the flowering stage until they've given you all the cuttings you require. Keep motherplants under 18–20 hours of light at all times in order to keep them from flowering and having to revert them back to the vegetative stage.

After a certain amount of time, you will need to replace your motherplants with new ones. If you want to keep the same characteristics, root a clone from your motherplant and vegetate it out to become your new mom. If you'd prefer to switch it up, start the process all over again with a new pack of seeds.

69

CHAPTER SIX

Cloning Success —Rooting Cuttings for Healthy Plants

The benefits of growing from clones instead of seeds include uniform growth, guaranteed female plants, and time saved while waiting for seedlings to sprout and mature. This chapter will show you how to take clones that will grow into healthy adult plants.

What are Clones & Why Grow Them?

Taking clones—or the process of cutting off a growing branch of a motherplant and forcing roots to grow from the cut end, in order to multiply one into many—isn't a technique invented by pot farmers. Since the earliest days of agriculture, people have looked for alternate ways to propagate plants without using seeds.

Clones are exact replicas of the plants they were taken from, so the benefit to cannabis horticulturalists is the elimination of the element of chance. You know exactly what you're going to get, so you can get a uniform crop of your favorite plants. Clones are taken from motherplants or vegetating plants that haven't begun the flowering process. Growing shoots are cut from the parent plant and then roots are induced from the bare cut end. Once the cuttings have rooted they are ready to start the vegetative stage of growth.

It is true that seed crops tend to exhibit greater vigor than clones, but clones outperform seeds in the long run: because the canopy will be level, clones make the most efficient use of your space and the light available, and this results in larger harvests. Replicating many copies of one plant provides many benefits to growing a garden from seeds. Because most seedlings will vary in size and growth rates, with different phenotypes behaving in various ways, seed gardens tend to be uneven, with light levels optimum for some plants but less so for others. Rooted clones provide a level canopy, with every plant performing alike and benefiting from all light available. Growing from seeds also wastes valuable time for the germination process, resulting in fewer total harvests per year.

From a quality-control perspective, a superb motherplant can be the gift that keeps on giving. Females with guaranteed elite genetics continue producing clone after clone of strong and tasty plants for many years. The only drawback to cloning is that all of the cuttings will share susceptibilities to fungi or disease, so always remain vigilant and start new moms if you have any problems. Purchasing rooted clones from a dispensary can sometimes cause more problems than it solves, so take care to check the clones are pest- and fungus-free if you decide to go that route.

Cloning Success

Choosing a medium in which to root your cuttings is the first step. As long as it stays moist, warm, and airy, pretty much any one will do.

Because cannabis cuttings root best in warm conditions with high humidity, the cheap trays with clear plastic domes work remarkably well. In cool conditions, a heat mat should be placed underneath the trays to maintain optimum temperature and humidity (75 degrees Fahrenheit and 80 percent relative humidity is about right). No matter where and into what medium you plan to root your clones, keep warmth and high humidity on your priority list. Clones allowed to get cold or dry will perish quite quickly. Too much humidity can also cause mold and rot, so cut a hole or two in your clear plastic dome to allow some air movement and circulation.

Choose a growing shoot with at least three sets of leaves and make the cut just below a node (the place where the leaves meet the stem). Make the cut with a sharp non-serrated blade, and do so at about a 45-degree angle to ensure plenty of rooting area. Trim off the closest set of leaves to your cut so that you can get the stem into your medium.

Immediately immerse the cut end into rooting hormone and then firmly but gently push the cut end into your pre-moistened rooting medium. Some people like to rough up the bottom inch or so of the stem with the knife gently to create more roots, but it's not absolutely necessary. Within 8–14 days, you should see white roots poking out of the bottom of your chosen medium. You are now ready to transplant the rooted clones into their bigger containers for the vegetative stage of growth.

What You'll Need

- ✗ Sharp non-serrated blade or razorblade
- ✗ Propagation tray and clear plastic dome
- ✗ Electric heating pad (propagation mat)
- ✗ Preferred medium (rockwool, soil mix, coco coir, etc.)
- ✗ Rooting hormone (gel or powder)
- ✗ Fluorescent lighting
- ✗ pH-balanced (6.0–6.5) mild nutrient solution
- ✗ Thermometer/ hygrometer

Cloning
Step by Step

STEP 1
Select a motherplant
to clone

A healthy motherplant will provide
dozens of cuttings, each a genetic
duplicate of the mother. It's important
that the plants from which you take
your clones are not flowering so keep
them under at least 18 hours of light
per day.

STEP 2
Choose where to cut your clone

Assemble all of your materials and have everything prepared and laid out before making any cuts. You want to cut clones just below a node (where the leaf meets the stem). You want to take a cutting where there are at least three sets of leaves and at least 2–3 inches of stem above where you plan to cut.

STEP 3
Cut with a sharp blade

Use an alcohol-sterilized blade and slice the stem at a 45-degree angle to ensure the most surface area at the cut end. Avoid exposing the cut end to air for any length of time. Air bubbles in the stem (embolism) will greatly decrease your rooting rate. Trim the leaves from the node just above your cut end, leaving a smooth half-inch to an inch of bare stem.

STEP 4
Dip the cut end in powdered or liquid/gel rooting hormone

Rooting hormone containing fungicide promotes the development of roots while at the same time discouraging fungus and rot that can attack your vulnerable cuttings. They seal the cut tissue and begin immediately supplying mild vitamins and minerals essential for promoting root growth. Dip the plants and ensure that the gel or powder covers the cut end and some of the stem above it.

STEP 5
Insert the clone into your chosen growing medium

Immediately after immersing the cut end into rooting hormone, firmly but gently push the cut end into your pre-moistened rooting medium. Take care not to force, break, or bend the stem, but do ensure that it is securely in place in your medium at least an inch or so without reaching the bottom of the tray.

Hydroponic growers sometimes make their clones in just air, using a mist to induce rooting at the cut end hanging down into a reservoir.

STEP 6

Place clones under light (cover tray with a clear plastic lid)

Install cool fluorescent lighting a few inches above the tray lid. Relative humidity should be near 80 percent and temperature near 75 degrees Fahrenheit. Too much humidity can also cause mold and rot, so cut a hole or two in your clear plastic dome to allow some air movement and circulation. Place the heating pad underneath the tray (if required to retain the temperature). Keep your medium moist using a mild nutrient solution (quarter strength). Avoid allowing stagnant water to sit in the tray, but never allow your medium to dry out. Misting with plain water is helpful early on.

STEP 7

Rooted clones are ready to transplant into their growing medium

Cuttings in proper conditions should show roots between five days and two weeks. Once you see roots coming out of the bottom of your medium, you are ready to transplant your clones into larger containers and begin the vegetative stage of growth.

CHAPTER
SEVEN

Vegetative Growth Stage

Growing, pruning, training: this is the time to maximize your plants' foundations so that they will bear the biggest yields.

Building the Foundation

Cannabis grows in two stages: vegetative and flowering. During the vegetative stage, plants develop the leaves, stems, and branches that lay the groundwork for strong plants able to bear the weight of future flowers. Once a plant begins flowering, it stops growing branches and begins to form buds. Plants grown indoors under lights spend the first stage of their lives receiving 18–24 hours of light per day. This vegetative period naturally takes place in the summertime, so consider this if you're growing outside, and if you're growing indoors this is what you'll be simulating. The warmer temperatures and longer periods of light allow seedlings to establish the healthy roots, branches, and foliar growth necessary to produce lots of buds further down the road.

Some growers vegetate plants for more than a month in order to grow huge bushes in large containers. "Sea of Green" growers, on the other hand, limit this vegetative time to just a week or less—but compensate for smaller plants by growing a greater number, closely spaced. (And often, the results, in terms of the yield, will be very similar.) Either way, the plant will continue to grow in its vegetative state until it is triggered to flower.

Lighting & Feeding

Lighting

The vegetative stage has specific requirements for the lighting schedule and color spectrum. The first consideration is that you need to choose the right light for the space you have, so refer back to Chapter 1 to find out about your options.

Cool blue light works well for growing cannabis plants, especially during the vegetative stage, so look for lights that in the spectrum of about 5,000–6,500k. I highly recommend MH (metal halide) lights. LEDs can provide adequate light for plants while they're vegetating, but they won't give you the best yield when it comes to flowering. As with LEDs, fluorescent lights aren't ideal for a great harvest, but young plants and clones will do well enough under them and overheating is less of a problem.

Vegetating plants require a lot of light—at least 18 hours per day, and some growers keep the lights on 24/7. Because of this, if you need to limit your electricity consumption, LEDs or fluorescents may be more suitable for you than super-bright but power-hungry HID lighting.

Feeding

Fertilizing vegetative plants properly requires an understanding of their particular needs.

On the NPK rating scale, nitrogen (N) ratios come first, followed by potassium (P) and phosphorus (K). During the vegetative stage, use fertilizer with a high number at the beginning (e.g. 5-1-1) listed on the package or bottle. Healthy green leaves and new growth are a sign that nitrogen levels are good, but lightening or yellowing leaves point to a deficiency. Burned leaf tips indicate an overabundance of nitrogen and other nutrients, so scale back and flush your plants with plain water if you see leaf tips start to get crispy.

Cannabis plant roots need a wet and dry cycle, so apply water or nutrient solution only when necessary. Plants in containers that stay constantly wet will exhibit signs of overwatering such as drooping and falling leaves. As the plant and its root system grow bigger, it will need more and more water and nutrients at a more frequent rate.

It helps to oxygenate the water during this time with an aquarium-style air pump and air stones. Add your nutrients and mix thoroughly before testing the pH and adjusting it up or down if necessary. Also, remember not to use cold or hot water that will shock sensitive roots. Lukewarm (72 degrees Fahrenheit) nutrient solution is ideal.

Foliar Feeding

The vegetative stage of growth is the best time for foliar feeding; spraying the leaves of your plants with water or mild nutrient solution such as aerated compost tea or liquid kelp added to water. Plants are able to absorb elements directly through their stomata, making foliar feeding a great way to get trace elements directly to where they are needed.

Outdoors, foliar feeding is best done in the morning before the sun is at its highest point to avoid burning leaves or branches. In the middle of the daytime, hot sun and bright light can force the stomata to close up. Indoors, this means you should foliar feed during the first hour or so that your lights are on. Avoid spraying closer to nighttime, or the dark cycle, as the liquid won't have time to absorb and will linger on the leaves, creating the perfect situation for molds to develop. Foliar feeding can be done every four days to a week during the vegetative stage.

Foliar feeding has the added benefit of cleaning your leaves of any dust that could be hindering the ability to take in light. It also discourages most pests from making a permanent home out of your plants. Be sure to spray both the tops and the undersides of leaves for full absorption.

Top Tips for Foliar Feeding

× Never foliar feed indoors without first protecting your light source from the mist.

× Cease foliar feeding at about two weeks into flowering to avoid issues with bud rot.

85

Transplanting Step by Step

"The bigger the root, the bigger the fruit," they say, so once a plant is established it's time to upgrade the size of your container to increase your future yield, particularly if your plants are root-bound.

It's not advised to transplant during the flowering stage because it can take up to a week for the plant to recover from the shock of transplantation. If you think you need to upgrade your plants' containers, it's ideal to do it now, during the vegetative stage, for best results.

Taking the time and care to transplant your plants properly will cause less stress and keep them growing happily, so it's worth the effort.

What You'll Need

× Sharp non-serrated blade or razorblade

× Propagation tray and clear plastic dome

× Electric heating pad (propagation mat)

× Preferred medium (rockwool, coco coir, etc.)

× Rooting hormone (gel or powder)

× Fluorescent lighting

× pH-balanced (6.0–6.5) mild nutrient solution

× Thermometer/ hygrometer

STEP 1
Prepare the new container

Have the pots you're transplanting into ready and waiting. Fill the new container about halfway with your growing medium, leaving space for the root ball and medium from your existing plants.

STEP 2
Wet the soil

Thoroughly wet the medium in your plant's existing container. This will keep it from falling apart when you remove the plant from its pot.

STEP 3
Remove the plant from its pot

Invert the plant upside down and gently try to remove it from the container. You may need to lightly tap on the bottom of the pot, or use your hand to loosen the pot from the medium. Make sure to hold the plant as you remove it—place your hand flat with the stem between your fingers so that you can hold it as it comes out of the pot.

STEP 4
Put the plant in its new pot

Gently place the plant, root ball down, into the new container and situate it into the medium.

STEP 5
Fill up the pot

Fill up the remaining space in the container with your grow medium and tamp it down.

STEP 6
Just add water

Help your plant settle into its new home by watering it with plain pH-balanced water.

Pinching, Pruning, & Training for Bigger Yields

Several techniques can be employed during the vegetative stage to produce more branches at canopy level, which can dramatically increase your later harvest. If you have limited space to grow, or if you're restricted in the number of plants you can grow, careful pruning will be a real benefit to you.

It can be as simple as trimming the tops off growing shoots in order to increase the number of future branches, but there are different ways to prune selectively, of which you can employ any combination to suit your needs. Once a plant has three or more nodes, you can begin the pruning process.

Training

Some growers "train" branches by weighing or tying them down. This has two advantages: it increases the surface area that light can reach, and it turns secondary branches into main, bud-bearing tops. Bushier plants produce greater yields than Christmas tree-shaped plants with one main cola. A sinker, like those used for fishing, works great to weigh down a main branch without having to cut it. Once the branch sags below lower branches, a signal is sent to the lower branches that they are no longer subordinate to a main top, and they can each become a dominant branch, thus raising your future harvests significantly.

If any branches are threatening to reach the light, bend them or tie them down to keep them from burning. A trellis system constructed from chicken wire at canopy level (aka the ScrOG or "Screen of Green" system detailed opposite) will further spread out bud sites and increase your yields considerably.

Pruning Lower Growth

You can prune to increase the number of potential bud sites on your plant and you can also prune to make your plant more efficient. Since almost all of the light in your grow room is absorbed by the canopy, the lower levels of foliage don't contribute to the yield but they still require energy to grow. Many growers trim these lower leaves and branches of their plants, resulting in lollipop-shaped plants.

Stripping the lower parts of your plants bare also helps with air circulation in your grow space, and makes it easy to check on what's happening at floor level—including monitoring sitting water or irrigation channels, and cleaning up old, dead growth.

Pruning for Increased Yields & Better Shape

You can use pruning to turn what would naturally be a tall, skinny plant with one main cola into a short, bushy one with several. This involves cutting or pinching branches just above a node where two new shoots will emerge. If you stay on top of this process, you'll end up with plants that look like small bushes, with plenty of bud sites but not a lot of stretching or big gaps between nodes. This is the efficient way to get big yields out of small spaces, but by pruning, your vegetating time will increase, so factor that into your schedule.

Green Screen

Some growers maximize yield by using the Screen of Green (ScrOG), a derivative of the Sea of Green (SOG) method in which premature flowering is forced in small, young plants. With the ScrOG method, the branches of your plants are spaced through a horizontal wire or string grid to efficiently reach as much light as possible. Much like the art of bonsai, young twigs are trained as they grow to fill a desired space.

By the time the plant is ready to flower, an even canopy extends across the entire closet's width. Your plants will need an additional week in the vegging chamber for the ScrOG method because they'll need more time to fill out. By trimming off the lower branches that don't fall within a light's optimal range for growth, you also force your plants to divert all their energy into the best buds.

As the growing shoots approach the trellis, bend them to fill the empty holes in the canopy. When they start the flowering process, leave them alone until it's time to harvest. Take care when removing the branches from the trellis not to damage the delicate trichome glands on the string or wire.

Remove yellow, burnt, and damaged leaves. Don't leave them on the plants or on the floor or they'll become a breeding ground for pests, molds, and diseases.

When Not to Prune

Don't prune at all in the lead-up to the flowering season. Pruning damages the plant, so energy that should be spent developing nice big healthy buds will instead be used for healing. This is when pruning is just counterproductive.

Some novices go overboard removing leaves, thinking they're doing their plants a favor. They're not—those leaves are needed for photosynthesis, to provide fuel to the whole plant. There's an argument for removing leaves when they're causing significant shade, and when they're old or dead, which you'll recognize because they become frail and yellow. But as a general rule, do it as little as possible.

Do You Need to Prune?

Some growers advocate not pruning at all. Pruning slows down your grow schedule and risks damaging plants, either through doing a bad job or by introducing diseases and pests. The need to prune will also depend on the space you have available and what strain you're growing—*indica*-dominant strains, for example, tend grow slower than *sativas*, so ruthless pruning of the former can set you back.

Pruning
Step by Step

While pruning can result in a harvest many times larger than would be possible if you let your plants grow the way nature intended, you can also damage your plants if you don't get it right. That's why it's important to do it with care and attention.

It's wise not to prune until you have some experience growing, so that you know how cannabis grows naturally. Bear in mind the growing characteristics of different strains—*indicas* grow slower than *sativas*, so you'll need to factor in different amounts of time to let them recover. Do your research first!

Finally, don't cut corners by using dirty tools. Have a set of tools reserved just for your indoor grow space, and clean the blades between uses. Like with human flesh, a wound, such as you're making in the pruning process, is a weak point when it comes to disease and infections, and careless pruning is a good way to spread these through your whole garden. On the other hand, pruning can be a good time to inspect your plants thoroughly for signs of illness, so it goes both ways.

What You'll Need

- ✗ Sharp, clean non-serrated blade or razorblade
- ✗ Sharp, clean scissors
- ✗ Sterilizing solution for blades (such as rubbing alcohol)
- ✗ String, clips, or ties for training
- ✗ Weights or sinkers (such as those used for fishing) for training
- ✗ Stakes, trellis, etc., to tie branches on to
- ✗ pH-balanced (6.0–6.5) water or nutrient solution

STEP 1
Topping—cut the top growth

Snip off the tip of a branch just above two new shoots to divert energy to the two lower shoots. You can use your fingers to pinch off the tender new growth (hence why this technique is sometimes called "pinching"), which some say is less damaging to the plant.

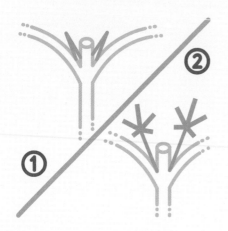

STEP 2
New shoots grow

After you've trimmed the top, you'll see the two new shoots begin to develop.

STEP 3
Branches develop

The shoots grow into new branches. Keep pinching selectively and your plant will grow into a bushy shape with the space well used and plenty of places for buds to grow. Stop pinching a couple of weeks before flowering to allow your new branches to develop and grow strong.

STEP 4
Fimming

"Fimming" is a technique very closely related to topping. Instead of cutting the stem of a branch, however, you cut the material of the new growing shoot. Cut about two thirds of the way down and you'll see a return of up to four new branches out of one. Not bad!

STEP 5
Give your plant some TLC

Pruning is stressful for your plants, so make sure to keep them well watered, and always allow enough time for recovery before your next pruning session.

CHAPTER EIGHT

Flowering Growth Stage
—Building Buds

The onset of flowering begins the final stage of growth during which the plant forms buds, starting from the tips of the branches and eventually filling out the entire branch with blooms.

Lighting for Flowering Plants

Flowering requires a strict 12-hours-on/12-hours-off lighting regimen with an uninterrupted dark period. Outdoors, as they would grow wild, this period would take place in the winter months when days are naturally shorter. Indoors, you, the grower, choose when to begin the flowering period by changing the setting on your light timer. Be sure to invest in a reliable timer. Cheaper ones are prone to failure and any variation in the light/dark cycle can cause problems with your plants, where the best outcome is a delay to your schedule as you lure them back out of vegetating to flowering, and the worst outcome is stress-induced hermaphrodism. Remember: never interrupt the dark cycle with any light! In an emergency, you can use a special light with a green bulb that won't register as light to the plant, but in all other circumstances, let the plants sit in full darkness for the full 12 hours per day that they need.

If the 12-hour dark period remains uninterrupted, the plant will shift from producing upward and outward growth and begin to form flowers, which eventually turn into the bud clusters that we prize. This transition, however, is gradual, and the plant will continue to stretch vegetatively for the first several weeks of the flowering phase. The hybrids typically grown by most cultivators flower for 45–65 days, but some pure *sativas* have been known to flower over periods of three months or more.

The ideal lighting system for the flowering period is a high-pressure sodium (HPS) lamp, reflector, and ballast. The wattage is decided by the size of the space in which you are growing, as well as your ability to remove excess heat from that space. A 250- or 400-watt HPS should serve beginners nicely (see page 19 for more information on lighting setupsp).

Depending on the wattage, lights should be between 18 and 24 inches away from plant tops. Lower or raise the lights or the plants to avoid making the plants stretch to reach the light or burning sensitive plant tops.

Temperature at canopy level during flowering should never exceed 80–85 degrees Fahrenheit to avoid slowing flower growth and degrading the essential oils. Try to keep temperatures as close to 70 degrees Fahrenheit as you can get for best results.

Feeding Flowering Plants

During the flowering stage, pot plants' nutritional requirements are quite different to the vegetative stage. Flower production requires less nitrogen but increases in phosphorus, potassium, calcium, and some micronutrients.

The First Two Weeks

The first two weeks after you've switched the lighting schedule are the transitional period and, because flowers haven't yet formed, a mild nutrient solution is best.

This period is referred to as the "stretch" period because the plants will continue to grow in what looks like a vegetative style, forming leaves and reaching for the light, until the nodes begin to get closer and closer together, and the first flowers finally begin to form at the tip of each branch.

After Two Weeks

After two weeks, nutrient requirements increase. This middle flowering period, approximately 2–6 weeks on average but depending on the strain, of course, is the time that the flower bracts will stack as flowers will do most of their forming. This is also when the trichomes form and develop, filling with essential oils containing cannabinoids, terpenes and flavonoids. Savvy growers use additives such as Cal/Mag and organic bloom boosters such as bat guano during this period to boost the size and resin production of their flowers.

Avoid overfeeding! Burned leaf tips are the first sign of plants that have an overabundance of nutrient added. Check your runoff water for fluctuations in PPM (parts per million—the measure of mineral solubles in water), as well as pH levels, which may be decreasing your roots' ability to take in nutrients. Adjust accordingly by flushing overfed plants and buffering pH in your next watering regimen. Don't foliar feed during the flowering stage as it can encourage mold and bud rot.

Make sure flowering branches don't bend too low, sag, or break by using a trellis or by attaching them to secure stakes to hold them up. Branches that are far from the light will not fill out with flowers the way they should and need to be supported. Remove lower branches and leaves that aren't getting enough light below the dense canopy.

Six Weeks +

As the flowering period begins to come to an end, bud production slows. Fan leaves begin to fade in color from bright green to yellow, the white hairs protruding from the bracts/calyxes begin to turn red and shrivel, and essential oils within the trichomes go from clear to cloudy.

Flushing

Removing excess fertilizer salts from your plants prior to harvest will give you clean-burning buds with proper flavor and scent.

Flushing should be accomplished within the last two weeks of flowering by using plain pH-balanced water instead of nutrient solution in order to leach out any remaining minerals from your growing medium and your plants. Pour the water until it flows heavily out of the bottom of your containers during this time.

You may see some yellowing of the leaves or other fall colors developing but don't be alarmed: this is a good thing and simply means that your quest to reduce chlorophyll and other unnecessary elements trapped within your buds has been successful.

The reason for flushing will reveal itself when it's time to consume your cannabis. Well-flushed pot will burn to a clean white ash, whereas unflushed buds burn dark like a piece of coal and need to be continually relit. When marijuana is properly flushed, it reveals all of the subtle scents and flavors without any harshness to interfere with the experience. Most growers, and particularly commercial growers, don't flush their plants properly for the full amount of time necessary to achieve the best results.

CHAPTER
NINE

The Proper Harvest
—When & How to Take
Plants Down

You've come too far to mess things up now. Harvesting the right way at the appropriate time ensures the highest quality in your finished product.

When to Harvest

There are a couple of telltale signs that indicate when your buds are getting ripe. One of the first things you'll probably notice is the flowers' smell becoming more intense (so make sure you're prepared with carbon filters to neutralize odors—see Chapter 1). Now you may observe the pistils (the little hair-like strands) turning from white to red/brown and curling in. But the most accurate way to decide when to cut down your bounty requires a close look at the glandular trichomes on the surface of your finishing flowers.

A loupe or magnifying glass will enhance your ability to examine the trichome gland heads up close. As your plants continue to flower, these tiny resin glands will become more and more bulbous. When they are nearing maturity, they will begin to go from clear to cloudy, and then, eventually, they will take on an amber color.

The ideal time to harvest is when the majority of the glands have become cloudy but not yet amber. A few will still be clear and some will be amber but if you've looked around closely and have determined that most of the trichome heads are cloudy, you are ready to take down your plants. Depending on the size and strain of your plants, you might want to harvest over a period of time, as the buds closest to the light are likely to fully ripen before the lower buds.

Like the story of the turtle and the hare, growing great marijuana is not a race won by sprinting. Resist the temptation to take down your plants too early or rush through the harvesting process. Buds that are plucked too soon or quick-dried are far inferior to those that are allowed to go the distance. As legendary cannabis breeder Soma always says, "If you think it's ready, wait a week!"

Different Harvests for Different Highs

As your buds ripen, their chemical consistency changes. With an extra level of precision, you can control the effect:

× Harvesting early, when most of the trichomes remain clear, doesn't allow the THC content to reach its peak. The result is a heady high with little psychoactive effect.

× Harvesting when most of the trichomes are cloudy, with some clear and some amber, means the THC content is at its peak. This is usually the balanced ideal you're looking for.

× Harvesting when most of the trichomes are turning amber results in CBD-rich buds for a heavy, physical effect. By this time, the THC will have begun to degrade.

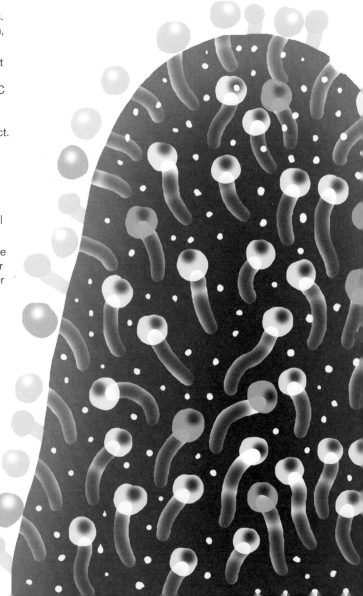

How to Harvest

Before getting started, prepare your trimming space with a clean table, small clipping scissors or snips, and a comfortable chair. You'll want plenty of light to be able to see what you're doing. If you have trusted friends helping you, add trimming equipment and chairs for them as well. Make sure they understand the importance of keeping quiet about your operation. Your security, as well as theirs, depends on resisting any urge to brag about the work being done. It will take one experienced trimmer about two to four hours per pound so choose helpers wisely (if you need them at all).

Your trimming and drying area need to be kept cool. Temperatures over 70 degrees Fahrenheit will heat the essential oils and release some of the scents and flavors that you're trying to capture and save. The less you volatilize now, the more your finished buds will retain their terpene profile.

Handle With Care

Harvest and trim gently to avoid damaging the delicate trichome heads that contain the oils. Avoid exposing your harvested branches to bright light, strong wind or high humidity.

The best time to harvest is in the "morning," just before the lights come on. This is when essential oil content is at its peak. Use sharp pruning shears to cut the plant at its base. You can trim smaller plants whole or cut larger ones into easier-to-manage branches, and you might want to harvest a plant branch by branch if the buds aren't ripening evenly.

Trimming

Leaves must be removed from your flowers either before or after drying. This manicuring process ensures that your buds smell, taste, and burn as they should. Whether you do it before or after drying is a matter of personal preference, but I recommend doing it before—it's easier, you're less likely to damage the trichomes, and you tend to end up with neater results.

The first step is to remove the large fan leaves. These don't contain much that's of any use, so you can just dispose of them. Then trim the smaller leaves around the bud, reserving any that look resinous. Now trim any secondary leaves (known as "sugar" leaves for their sparkly coating of trichomes) that stick out from the buds.

The closer to the flowers that you trim, the less leaf you'll be smoking later, so take your time and try to cut big leaves at their base near the stem. Remember to keep any resinous leaf trimmings for making hashish extractions and cannabis butter. You can even juice them for some amazing health benefits!

Periodically, you will need to clean your trimming equipment and that's the time to take a break and try some "scissor hash." Before you scrub the scissors with rubbing alcohol and a rag or paper towel, scrape as much of the sticky residue off the blades and pack a bowl. This is some of the strongest and spiciest smoke you will ever try, and it makes all the meticulous and sometimes boring busywork more fun. Stay vigilant and try to keep these breaks short; they do have a tendency to extend further than planned.

Harvesting & Trimming Step by Step

Harvesting and trimming is a time- and labor-intensive process. But having spent all this time nurturing your plants to give the best yield, it's worth making the effort to do the best job you can with your valuable harvest.

Work rigorously and methodically, following this simple step-by-step guide.

What You Need

- A clean table and comfortable chair.
- Overhead and directional lighting as required.
- Sharp, strong pruning clippers.
- Small scissors or trimming clippers.
- Trays for untrimmed buds, trimmed buds, and offcuts.
- Rubbing alcohol to clean scissors as they gum up.
- String or coat-hangers to hang the branches for drying.
- A fan to circulate air in the drying area (do not point it directly at the buds).
- Jars to cure and store your pot.

STEP 1
Cut the first cola

Start with the top cola and cut just below the first branch that joins it. Trim the fan leaves and sugar leaves as closely as you can to the flower without damaging it. Place all the cut branches into a tray, ready for processing.

STEP 2
Work from the top down

Continue cutting the branches off just below the next branch from the top. You might find that the buds haven't fully ripened on the lower branches, in which case you can leave these branches attached to the plant until the buds are ready. Trim off fan leaves and sugar leaves as above. Be sure to remove all petioles (leaf stems) where they meet the plant stem—you can have mold problems if they're left attached.

Chapter Nine

STEP 3
Trim & manicure

Trim the fan leaves from each branch and discard. Trim the small, fingered leaves from each branch, discarding any that aren't resinous. Carefully trim the single-fingered sugar leaves as close as you can to the petiole. Reserve all your "trimmings" in a separate tray for later use. Put your processed bud branches into their own tray.

STEP 4
Hang the branches to dry

Cutting your branches in the way described Step 1 means they each form their own hooks. They can be hung on a line or wire hangers.

Dry slowly over several days, with plenty of air circulation and a temperature not exceeding 70 degrees Fahrenheit, for best results. You'll know when the branches are properly dry because they will snap rather than bend.

STEP 5
Cut to size

Carefully cut each individual bud off the main branch.

STEP 6
Store & cure

Place your buds into airtight containers—preferably glass—and store in a dark place for the curing process. Pack as many buds into this space as possible without squashing and damaging them.

Drying

Branches laden with buds must be hang dried in a cool, dark place for the proper amount of time before they enter the curing process.

Always hang your plants to dry in a dark room or closet. Humidity levels in the drying area should be around 50–60 percent and temperature should be between 60–70 degrees Fahrenheit. It's a good idea to have a fan circulating air in the room but not directly blowing on the buds. Within a week or so, depending on ambient humidity, the buds will be crispy on the outside and ready for the curing process.

By cutting branches in the way shown on the previous pages, each becomes its own hook to hang on the drying

line. If you don't have a natural hook, use string or clothes pins instead. Make sure not to crowd the branches in order to facilitate air movement around the buds and reduce the risk of mold. Never dry buds or branches by laying them down on a drying rack.

Some people reverse the trimming and drying process and hang their plants without manicuring them at all. They choose to trim the leaves off the buds after drying the plants whole. This may be a bit more time-consuming, but the finished product inevitably dries slower—and slow drying makes for tastier pot.

Curing

Curing almost-dried flowers in glass jars results in connoisseur-quality cannabis that accentuates the qualities of a strain.

Buds that have gone through the process of curing aren't really "dry." There is still moisture deep within them and that is why curing is so important. Starches and chlorophyll in the plant need to be "sweated" out to reduce the harsh taste of un-cured pot. Curing is a delicate balance between moisture and dryness: too wet and the buds will mold; too dry and they crumble into dust.

When the hanging branches begin to get crispy and the stems snap when bent, trim them down to individual buds and place them into completely sealed, airtight, opaque glass jars. Moisture from inside the buds will spread outward in no time at all, and the seemingly dry nuggets you put in will soon be wet again.

Opening the jars for a few minutes several times daily releases the built-up humidity and replenishes the air inside. Slowly but surely, evaporation will lower the moisture levels in the jar and the buds will "crisp up." Some growers use paper bags for this process but that is ill-advised and imparts an unpleasant flavor and odor.

Well-dried and cured pot is sweet and smooth with n harshness. If a joint burns evenly and the ashes are wispy and white, the herb is well cured. Poorly cured pot won't stay lit and the ashes will be dark and crumbly like charcoal.

Advanced growers often push the limits to how long they go without opening their jars. They want their buds to ferment in the air that's left in the jar as oxygen becomes depleted and gases build up. Buds cured this way taste very sweet and are imparted with subtle flavors not unlike a fine aged wine. However, the longer the flowers stay closed inside jars, the more of a risk of mold, so use this method with caution!

Storage

Storing your pot correctly preserves its quality so that you can enjoy it for a long time to come. It's up to you to protect your precious pot from natural enemies, such as mold, humidity, and exposure to light.

Plastic baggies should never be used for long-term pot storage. First of all, the buds will get crushed with any movement of the bag in your pocket, bookbag, or purse. This creates a powdery mess of shake at the bottom of the bag and breaks apart the flowers you're hoping to keep intact. Also, odors permeate easily out of plastic baggies, even sealable ones. Aside from the issues with security and stealth, this permeation is also indicative of your buds losing scents and flavors, both obvious and subtle, to the air.

If odors are getting out, that means moisture is released as well, resulting in dried-out buds that lack flavor and burn harshly and unevenly. A small amount of moisture is essential in long-term cannabis storage: buds that dry out completely taste unpleasant and are less potent.

Find some airtight mason jars, preferably opaque, and do not overstuff them. Be sure to select an appropriate size for the amounts of cannabis you plan to store. You don't want too much space in your jar because extra space means extra air, and your buds will dry out faster.

Never store cannabis in a refrigerator or freezer. Temperatures and humidity levels inside fridges fluctuate too much and aren't set at ideal levels to begin with. The freezer is even worse, as temperatures below freezing can separate trichomes from your pot. Also remember, heat rises and heat will quickly dry out your cannabis, so don't store your jars in cabinets that are above appliances that produce heat like an oven, microwave, or refrigerator. Keep your jars in a dark, cool, dry place such as a closet or drawer and you'll be enjoying your homegrown cannabis at peak potency and flavor for months if not years to come.

CHAPTER TEN

Pests, Fungi, Molds, & Deficiencies—Prevention, Detection, Identification, & Controls

Discovering problems quickly and treating them properly to control or eliminate them is essential to keeping your garden alive and thriving.

Pests

Many types of bug can attack and destroy your plants unless you fight back. You have some different options which vary depending on the critter.

Integrated Pest Management (IPM)

The best technique for managing an issue with pests involves various natural mechanisms. You need to employ several tactics, including occasionally spraying plants with natural repellents like neem or rosemary oil, introducing predators, and misting leaves with organic insecticidal soap mixed with water.

Prevention

Always keep all areas of your growing space clean. There can be no pooling water on the floor or dead leaves lying around. These become homes and breeding grounds for pests and molds. Remove yellow leaves from your plants, because they are no longer converting light into energy and act only as an invitation to pests. This is the reason that the sticky traps growers hang up are yellow: it is the color of decay, and bugs of all kinds are drawn to yellow surfaces, because these weakened places become a base from which to attack the rest of a healthy plant.

Organic vs Chemical: Pest Control

A bone of contention among growers is the use of potentially harmful pesticides. Some swear by pyrethrum "bombs" and chemical sprays, while others lean toward natural repellents or predatory insects and nematodes that fight and destroy the pests we hate, such as spider mites, whiteflies, and thrips. Most agree that the latter are safer for the finished product than the former, but growers sometimes find themselves quite overwhelmed by pest issues. Many more resort to "nuclear" tactics than seem to admit.

A combination of good grow room hygiene practices, such as checking the undersides of leaves daily and occasionally rinsing them with a mild pest treatment, will keep most insect attacks at bay. Scrupulous vigilance against pests will reward you in other ways, like the discovery of a pH problem or a nutrient-burned plant that you otherwise might have missed.

My recommendation is to use the mildest and least damaging tactics possible, not only in pest control, but also in terms of nutrient administration, sanitation, and in all areas of plant care generally. Well-cared-for plants produce better-tasting pot. Keep it simple, and keep it green!

On the following pages we'll look at some of the most common pests that afflict cannabis, and how to detect and control their populations.

Spider mites

Spider mites are a tiny but hugely destructive pest that suck the chlorophyll out of leaf cells. Mites must be dealt with immediately upon discovery with an aggressive program of pest control. They multiply so quickly, you'll find a many-pronged approach most effective in beating back these costly and annoying pests.

Always check the undersides of fan leaves as a preventative daily precaution. Don't forget that one tough-to-reach plant in the back corner of the room—infestations usually begin in the overlooked places, so make sure to regularly check your plants and their surroundings, especially the surface of the growing medium.

During the vegetative or the beginning stages of flowering, if you see the early signs of spider mites—yellow or white dots on the leaf tops and tiny black moving dots underneath—immediately begin your war with the pesky bugs. Use a neem-oil-based spray and mist your plants liberally on the tops and bottoms of the leaves, as well as the stalks and soil surface. Mites reproduce faster in hotter temperatures, so cool your room at any sign of infestation.

Whiteflies

Whiteflies resemble tiny moths and feed on the underside of plant leaves, draining them of moisture, slowing growth, and leaving telltale slimy marks on the tops of the leaves. They enjoy moist conditions, so overwatering and high humidity can bring upon outbreaks or exacerbate an existing infestation.

One effective method for dealing with whiteflies is the introduction of predators such as green lacewing larvae and ladybugs. These can be ordered through the mail or purchased at nurseries. Remember that it may take multiple well-timed applications to truly control harmful insect populations.

Thrips

Thrips, a tiny cigar-shaped insect species, are a plague on cannabis plants second only to spider mites. They pierce the cell walls of leaves and drain them of their essential fluids. They leave behind a shiny trail on leaf tops as if they were tiny slugs. In addition to sucking out the valuable juices inside the plant, they also carry and transmit diseases known as tospoviruses that cause necrotic spots and can eventually destroy a whole garden. Thrips are very difficult to completely eradicate, but it isn't that hard to control their populations and keep them at a minimal level of damage.

There are predators that will take care of thrips—you can buy slow-releasing sachets of beneficial mites that will tackle thrips (*Amblyseius cucumeris*) and spider mites (*Amblyseius californicus*)—but I'd like to share a personal recipe. Put three drops of neem oil into a quart of warm water plus two drops of dish soap. Shake it up and spray it all over the leaves, top and bottom. Also be sure to dip a cotton swab into this formula and use it to get between leaf ribs and hard-to-reach spots where mature thrips will run to and hide, such as where leaves meet the stem. It won't kill right away, rather it makes the adults infertile and interrupts the breeding cycle. Spray this solution once a week to keep populations in check.

Root Aphids

Root aphids reproduce so rapidly that some growers say they're "born pregnant and die pregnant." They're also often misdiagnosed as fungus gnats, and traditional treatments such as Azamax and Gnatrol won't work to treat them. Root aphids have been found in every kind of growing medium from soil to coco to hydroponic ones such as rockwool and grow rocks (expanded clay pellets). They've even been seen in aeroponic and DWC systems where roots dangle in mist and nutrient solution only.

Getting rid of root aphids requires a combination of efforts. Rotate your pest control regimen daily using neem oil, pyrethrins, and other organic insecticides, and be sure to treat the medium as well as the plant. There's a promising product called Botanigard, made of a fungus, that attacks aphids, whiteflies, and thrips.

Fungus Gnats

These small black flies are truly annoying and can prove to be expensive over time. Their larvae feed on plant roots, causing damage to the plant if left unchecked. Their presence is a surefire indicator of overwatering.

Yellow sticky traps will help control the problem. The gnats are attracted to the yellow color and many of the already flying mature ones will end up stuck to the traps when hung at plant level. To get rid of the younger larvae, drench the soil with a biological larvicide such as Gnatrol twice weekly for one month in conjunction with a diluted neem oil spraying of your soil mix surface. Their life cycle is less than eight days, so you should be rid of them shortly.

The best way to avoid the problem of fungus gnats altogether is to not provide a comfortable home for them. They prefer the top layer of your pots to be moist and warm. Instead, bottom-feed your plants using a wick system or purchase some self-watering containers specially made to water from the bottom up. The plant roots will pull up only what they need, and the top layer will be much less desirable real estate for fungus gnats to move in and lay their eggs.

Fungi & Mold

Some plant diseases, such as the dreaded powdery mildew, originate from the air and thrive in humid environments.

Powdery Mildew & Other Fungal Diseases

The fungal disease known as powdery mildew (PM for short) is a true plague on the marijuana farmer, indoors and out. It starts off looking like a fine white dust and is most likely to appear first on young vegetation. Left untreated, it will consume the whole plant, buds and all, and can quickly spread to infect entire gardens. Once diagnosed, PM must be tackled swiftly and aggressively, before it totally ruins your harvest.

Pythium, fusarium, anthracnose, and botrytis are all different kinds of fungal diseases that can cause serious problems from damping off (a disease that destroys seedlings) to leaf blight to bud rot to sudden plant death.

Fungi thrive in wet conditions, so the best way to prevent them is to control the level of moisture in the air and in your growing medium. Once a fungus is identified, reduce your ambient humidity to below 50 percent and increase circulation and ventilation. Don't reuse growing mediums and always use sterile tools when cutting any live plant material for any reason. Avoid overwatering your plants and don't allow any standing water to remain in your grow space. Spray with fungicides or employ a sulphur burner if necessary, but both of these are to be avoided unless a last resort. Some strains are more resistant than others to PM and other molds.

Nutrient Deficiencies

Underfed plants exhibit a variety of symptoms depending on which nutrient compound is lacking. Identify and treat unhealthy deficiencies to avoid setbacks in growth.

Always check the pH of your growing medium before diagnosing a deficiency. Fluctuations in acidity and alkalinity affect the roots' ability to uptake nutrients. Even with an abundance of a particular nutrient, that nutrient can be locked out and unavailable to the plant. A misdiagnosis of deficiency, and the addition of more nutrient solution, will only cause more serious problems for the grower.

Once carefully diagnosed, treat a deficiency by adding nutrient solution containing the missing element.

Nitrogen (N) Deficiency

Leaves become yellow starting at the tips of the lower, older leaves, progressing upward to the rest of the leaves. Growth eventually slows as leaves continue to yellow. If a nitrogen deficiency is left uncorrected, leaves will eventually turn brown, dry, and fall off the plant.

Phosphorus (P) Deficiency

When a phosphorus deficiency is present, the leaf tips of older leaves will darken and turn downward. Newer leaves will turn darker from the edges in. Red and purple stems and petioles are also a sign a plant is lacking phosphorus. Severe deficiency leads to dark blotches on leaves, growth slows to a crawl and then stops.

Potassium (K) Deficiency

A lack of potassium shows first as burned leaf tips and leaf edges, with those leaves eventually developing spots and curling up. Older leaves can turn red, form dead patches, and eventually die.

Calcium/Magnesium (CalMag)

These two micronutrients are the most common to be found lacking. A deficiency will show as dark green veins on fan leaves, with yellow patches between them starting at the petiole or node (where the leaf meets the stem). Another sign of deficiency is "taco

leaves," where leaves curl upward from the middle and develop rust spots and dark purple stalks.

Other Micronutrient Deficiencies

Deficiencies in trace nutrients such as sulfur, zinc, iron, manganese, and others can also occur frequently. They will express themselves in different ways, but the remedy is almost always simply to add more micronutrients into your watering solution.

CHAPTER ELEVEN

Concentrates, Edibles, Tinctures, & Topicals

Trimmed leaves and buds can be used and consumed in a multitude of ways, including concentrated into various forms of hash, added to foods, dissolved into alcohol or glycerine, and even applied to the body in lotions and creams.

Concentrates

Hashish

Hashish consists primarily of the pressed together resin glands that have been separated from female cannabis buds and leaves. Essentially, hashish is concentrated marijuana; nothing else need be (or should be) added or done than simply removing the trichome heads from their stalks, whether by dry sifting or using one of several ice-water extraction methods. The result of this hallowed and ancient process becomes a chunk of soft, pliable, oily, earthy hashish.

Traditionally hashish arrived from exotic locales like Morocco, Nepal, and India, but medical cannabis growers in the US now produce their own hash from otherwise discarded parts of each harvest, like fan leaves and trim.

Dry Sift

There are several things you can do with your sugar leaves. One of the simplest is to make dry sift. Dry sift is easy to make, melts well, and tastes amazing when free of impurities.

The simplest ways to achieve this is to sift the dried branches of mature female plants over a silkscreen, then gather and press together the "powder" that falls through using slight heat and some pressure. This is the more traditional version of hashish that you might find when traveling in Asia or the Middle East.

Different strains have different-sized trichome heads, so it will take a bit of trial and error to find the size of silkscreen that's best for just removing the heads. The more gland stalks and plant material that falls through your screen, the less likely your hash will be to melt. Potency is also lower when impurities are present in the hash.

Ice-Water Extraction

Ice-water extraction is a fairly recent and quite popular method for making hashish. Some people call the result of this method "bubble hash" or "ice wax." After harvest, leftover leaf and trim are combined with ice-cold water and agitated. The trichome heads freeze and fall through a screened bag into a series of finer screened bags. Each level of screen represents a different grade of hash. Ice-water extracted hash must be dried thoroughly to remove any water remaining and keep it from molding.

After drying, the paste crumbles and turns to a more sand-like consistency. When smoked, it can overpower the user and cause serious coughing fits. This type of product should only be used by a seasoned cannabis consumer. With bubblehash, remember to sip and not chug.

The best bubblehash is light brown or blond, and when heated will melt and form "full-melt domes" or large clear bubbles. Still-moist bubblehash, what I sometimes call "sizzle-hash," will pop and boil, but leaves a harsh, black coal ball behind in the bowl. Hash with a green tint contains large amounts of plant matter, which dilutes its potency and flavor. Hash that's gone stale will become brittle and lose its fragrance.

Butane Hash Oil (BHO)

I'm not going to suggest that you use butane or another explosive solvent to extract your trichomes because it is a dangerous process. Only experts in chemical extraction should attempt to make BHO, or butane hash oil. Too many amateurs are blowing themselves and their houses up for me to recommend this to anyone. Leave this dangerous process to trained chemists.

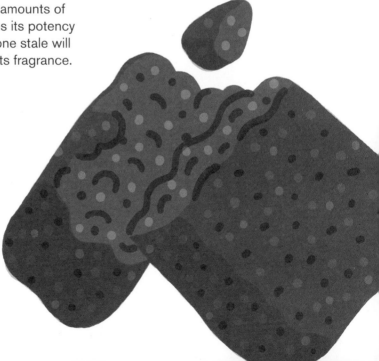

Edibles

Cooking with Cannabis

A fun and rewarding thing you can do is to cook with your sugar leaves. Adding pot to food has come a long way since space brownies. Virtually any food product can be infused with cannabis at varying levels of potency. Having slowly heated excess leaves and trim in unsalted butter or oil over a period of several hours, you can use that butter or oil to create a wide variety of edibles, both sweet and savory.

Keep in mind, the effects of cannabis-infused food can come on anywhere from a half hour to several hours after ingestion, and vary widely according to body weight, cannabis tolerance, and whether you're eating them on an empty stomach or after a large meal. Even blood sugar plays a role. So, to avoid an unwanted or unpleasant effect, I advice friends and strangers to either "bake your own," allowing you to carefully regulate dosage, or to rely on suppliers with a proven track record of consistency of product.

Cannabutter Recipe

As a rule, you'll want to use a quarter ounce of cannabis per stick of butter. Work out how much you want to make and get the quantities prepared before anything else.

Bake your cannabis in the oven at 220 degrees Fahrenheit for 30 minutes on a cookie sheet to decarboxylate it (that is, to activate the cannabinoids).

Melt the butter in a medium saucepan on your stovetop. Use the lowest heat and stir occasionally with a wooden spoon to stop it from burning. When the butter has melted, add the cannabis and simmer on the lowest heat for at least an hour.

When ready, strain the butter through cheesecloth over a bowl, to remove the particles of cannabis. Let the mixture cool in the fridge.

Tinctures

Cannabis tinctures are concentrations resulting from soaking leaf, or preferably buds or resins, typically in alcohol (although alternatives to alcohol-based tinctures do exist—see opposite). The extraction is usually administered using a dropper or a sprayer, and is most effective when taken under the tongue for quick absorption. Medicinal marijuana patients rave about the fast-acting pain-killing properties of tinctures when they are properly made and administered.

Making Alcohol Tincture

Start with 90 percent pure alcohol (190-proof Everclear works well) and soak your chosen dry bud or leaf in it at least overnight and up to a month if desired. The longer you leave it, the more potent your tincture will be.

Strain out the solids and store in a sealed dark-colored jar or bottle in a dark, cool place. For a more basic version, soak in a sweet liqueur such as brandy or flavored schnapps and use to dissolve in food or drink for slower absorption.

Making Glycerin Tincture

Bud breeder and medicinal marijuana proponent Subcool transcribed his recipe for a vegetable glycerin-based tincture perfect for patients. He advises using finely ground buds and soaking the powder in glycerin for two months before separating the solids with a 190-micron hash-straining bag. For dosage, he recommends 15ml added to unsweetened grape juice for a potent and pleasant body buzz. Migraine patients marvel at the efficacy of this tincture and recovering alcoholics rejoice at having an alternative to booze-based solutions.

Topicals

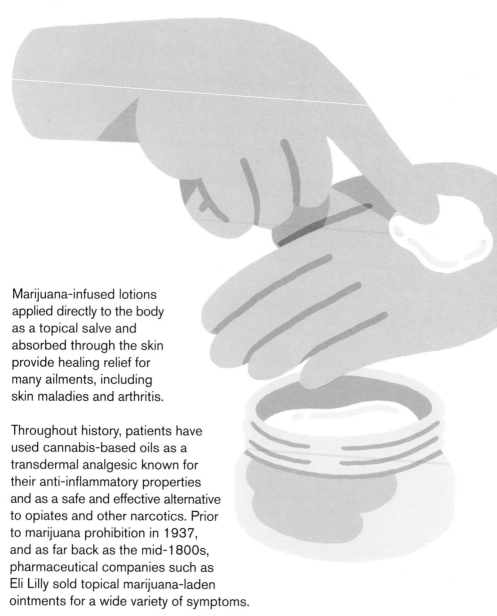

Marijuana-infused lotions applied directly to the body as a topical salve and absorbed through the skin provide healing relief for many ailments, including skin maladies and arthritis.

Throughout history, patients have used cannabis-based oils as a transdermal analgesic known for their anti-inflammatory properties and as a safe and effective alternative to opiates and other narcotics. Prior to marijuana prohibition in 1937, and as far back as the mid-1800s, pharmaceutical companies such as Eli Lilly sold topical marijuana-laden ointments for a wide variety of symptoms.

There are many marijuana-infused coconut oil applications available in dispensaries, and some dispensaries even offer a variety of oil-based products including lip balms and massage creams. These work to relieve sore muscles and joint pain, and have also shown promise in relieving the symptoms of arthritis and rheumatism, as well as skin ailments such as psoriasis, eczema, and burns.

Because the cannabinoids are absorbed through the skin, topical applications usually have less of a psychoactive effect and more of a pain-relieving quality in the body. This is perfect as an alternative for patients who prefer not to smoke or vaporize and for whom potent edibles prove too strong of a high.

Making a Cannabis Salve

As with making cannabutter, start by baking your cannabis in the oven at 220 degrees Fahrenheit for 30 minutes on a cookie sheet to decarboxylate it. For this recipe, use about a quarter of an ounce.

Heat a cup of coconut oil in a medium saucepan to a very low simmer and keep stirring. Add the cannabis and continue to stir for 30 minutes.

Strain the mixture through cheesecloth into a bowl. Add cup of warmed beeswax and let it cool.

Glossary

Aeroponic
A method of growing, in which nutrients are administered to bare roots via a mist.

Auto-flowering
A plant that flowers automatically regardless of photoperiod.

Ballast
A device to regulate electrical current, used with some lighting systems.

Bract
The leaf-like structure that forms just underneath a forming flower.

Cannabinoid
The chemical components of marijuana, such as THC and CBD, that produce a variety of effects on the human body

Calyx
A tear-shaped cluster of flower sepals.

Clone
An identical replica of a motherplant, cut off from the mom and rooted.

Cola
A stack of buds.

Curing
Sweating excess remaining moisture from buds after drying.

Dioecious
A plant with different and separate male and female specimens

Feminized
A type of seed that grows only female plants.

Flowering growth
The stage when plants bloom and form flower buds.

Flushing
Leaching out excess elements by flooding the root zone with plain water.

Foliar feeding
Misting a plant's leaves with water or mild nutrient solution.

Genotype
The stored genetic "footprint" held within the plant's DNA.

Hermaphrodite
A plant with both male and female flowers.

Hybrid
A strain that is a combination of *indica* and *sativa* genetics.

Hydroponic
A style of growing without using soil or soilless mix.

Indica
A short, stocky species of cannabis with wide leaves and a short flowering time.

Landrace
Original plant genetics from the place of origin.

Lumens
The total amount of light emitted by a source.

Medium
The substance chosen by the grower to support and sustain their root system (e.g. soilless mix, perlite, coco coir, peat moss etc.)

Motherplant
A female plant, kept in the vegetative stage, from which to take clones.

Node
The place where a leaf or branch meets the stem.

NPK
The ratio of nitrogen, phosphorus, and potassium in a nutrient solution

Organic
Growing without the use of concentrated chemical nutrient salts.

Parts per million (PPM)
A unit of measure for very minute concentrations.

Petiole
Leaf stem at the point where it meets the branch.

pH
The measure of acidity or alkalinity on a scale of 0–14.

Phenotype
A plant's observable expression of its genetic material within its environment.

Pistil
The white hair that protrudes from a female flower.

Pollen
Fine grains released by male flowers to pollinate females producing seeds.

Powdery mildew (PM)
A fungal disease that attacks cannabis leaves and plants.

Preflowers
Early signifiers of sex that begin show on nodes around the fourth week of vegetative growth.

Pruning
The selective trimming of leaves and branches to maximize efficient growth.

Reflector
A device used with lighting systems to maximize the amount of light in a space.

Reverse osmosis (RO)
A process that removes contaminants from water.

Sativa
A species of cannabis with a long flowering time and thin long leaves.

Screen of Green (ScrOG)
A trellising system using netting to spread growing shoots apart at canopy level.

Sea of Green (SoG)
A technique where flowering is induced after a minimal vegetative period to produce quick harvests.

Sepal
The outermost parts of the flower, which support and protect the petals.

Sinsemilla
Without seeds, meaning a female flower that hasn't been pollinated with male genetic material.

Tincture
A concentrated cannabis solution, usually using strong alcohol to extract the active chemical compounds.

Topical
A salve or lotion containing cannabis.

Training
The practice of bending and tying branches to achieve the most efficient spread of foliage.

Trichome
The tiny, clear, mushroom-shaped gland that contains essential oils.

Vegetative growth
The stage of growth during which plants grow leaves and branches.

Vigor
A quality of some plants expressed by quicker growth and increased hardiness.

Acknowledgments

First and foremost, my wife Sarah, whose love, patience, and support is unwavering. Thank you for a lifetime of wonderful experiences! I love you more than words can tell...

My son Alexander (Sasha). May your life be filled with joy and happiness! Always remember your sense of childlike wonder. A quote from your namesake: "The world amazed me, in that I saw it as I had when I was a child. I had forgotten the beauty and the magic and the knowingness of it and me."
- Alexander Shulgin

My mentors, Jorge Cervantes, Kyle Kushman, and Dr. Lester Grinspoon

My editors—Zara and Rachel—and everyone at Octopus, as well as illustrator Paul Layzell.

All of the freedom fighters working to end pot prohibition.

All of my *High Times* colleagues and contributors, past and present

My friends and family around the world.

Hampton Roads Publishing Company
. . . for the evolving human spirit

Hampton Roads Publishing Company publishes books on a variety
of subjects, including spirituality, health, and other related topics.

For a copy of our latest trade catalog, call (978) 465-0504
or visit our distributor's website at *www.redwheelweiser.com*.
You can also sign up for our newsletter and special offers by going to
www.redwheelweiser.com/newsletter/.